Working together for young children

D1079169

With 1994 de...
young chil... ...
firmly ba...
meet this...
to improv...
stressing...
and the car...

Working T...
facing you... ...is n...
social and ... ...t...
fields of he... ...
informatio... ...e
light of rec... ...
tinuity, co... ...nt
levels of car... ...s
directed a... ...

Working T... ...read... for
parents an... ...edu... n,
social work

Tricia Dav...
University...
Education. ...r m... ...n t...
early child... ...e ...
children ir... d
rights.

Working together for young children

Multi-professionalism in action

Edited by Tricia David

London and New York

First published in 1994
by Routledge
11 New Fetter Lane, London EC4P 4EE

Simultaneously published in the USA and Canada by Routledge
29 West 35th Street, New York, NY 10001

© 1994 Individual chapters: contributors

Typeset in Palatino by
NWL Editorial Services, Langport, Somerset

Printed and bound in Great Britain by
TJ Press (Padstow) Ltd, Padstow, Cornwall

British Library Cataloguing in Publication Data
A catalogue record for this book is available from the
British Library

Library of Congress Cataloging in Publication Data
A catalog record for this book is available from the
Library of Congress

ISBN 0–415–09247–7 (hbk)
ISBN 0–415–09248–5 (pbk)

Contents

List of figures and table   vii
List of contributors   ix
Preface and acknowledgements   xiii
Introduction   xv

1 What's so special about families?
  Tricia David   1

Part I Services for young children and their families

2 In sickness and in health
  Clare Blackburn   15

3 Childminders and children
  Judy Warner   26

4 Teachers and young children in educational
  establishments
  Cathy Nutbrown   35

5 Voluntary agencies, young children and their families:
  preschool playgroups
  Margaret Brown   47

6 Daycare and nursery education as a business.
  The private sector: an overview
  Vivienne Whittingham   66

Part II Children in need

7 Becoming a special family
  Elaine Herbert   81

8 When parents separate – having two homes
Erica De'Ath   93

9 Supporting 'children in need' – the role of the
social worker
Norma Baldwin and Christine Harrison   104

10 Young children in the care system
Sonia Jackson   119

11 Making a difference for children 'in need':
'educare' services
Tricia David   133

Part III Issues and implications

12 Young children in day nurseries and combined centres
run by the Social Services department –
practitioner research
Margy Whalley   145

13 Training to work with young children
Audrey Curtis   159

14 Coordinating provision – the story so far in one
local authority
Ann Sharp   170

15 Postscript. Supporting children and families –
an optimistic future?
Tricia David   182

Name index   185
Subject index   188

Figures and table

FIGURES

4.1   Links between people and agencies and the
        early-years teacher   44

9.1   The role of the social worker – ecological factors   108

TABLE

9.1   The relationship between the law, regulations
        and guidance   108

Contributors

Norma Baldwin worked in Probation and Social Services before moving to a teaching post at Warwick University in the Department of Applied Social Studies. Her main teaching and research areas are in child protection – particularly the development of preventive strategies in childcare, which take account of deprivation and of issues of race and gender. She is the author of *The Power to Care in Children's Homes* (Avebury Gower 1990) and, with J.Harris, R.Littlechild and M.Pearson, *Residents' Rights: a Strategy in Action in Homes for Older People* (Avebury Gower 1993).

Clare Blackburn worked as a nurse and health visitor prior to her present employment in higher education. She is currently a lecturer in the Department of Applied Social Studies at the University of Warwick. Her research is concerned with the effects of poverty and poor living circumstances on the health of families with children and the implications for health practitioners. Her publications include: *Poverty and Health: Working with Families* (Open University Press 1991); *Improving Health and Welfare Work with Families in Poverty* (Open University Press 1992); and, with Hilary Graham, *Smoking among Working Class Mothers: an information pack* (Department of Applied Social Studies, University of Warwick 1992).

Margaret Brown has recently resigned from the Preschool Playgroups Association, for which she had worked as a National and Regional Training and Development Officer since 1976. Her previous experience included work with children and parents as a nursery nurse, teacher, lecturer, social worker – and parent – in a variety of day and residential settings. Margaret has also worked in support of local and national projects with a number of voluntary agencies. She maintains, however, that her greatest learning experience has been in rearing her three sons.

Audrey Curtis has become widely known through her work as a Senior Lecturer at the London University Institute of Education and as an adviser to CATE (the Council for the Accreditation of Teacher Education); her publications, for example, *A Curriculum for the Preschool Child* (NFER-Nelson 1986); and for her work in OMEP (the World Organisation for Early Childhood Education), of which she is currently European Vice-President.

Tricia David is a Senior Lecturer in Education at the University of Warwick, where her research and teaching interests include policy relating to provision for young children and their families in different countries, children's rights and protection, and multi-professionalism. Her publications reflect these interests (e.g. *Under five – under-educated?* (Open University Press 1990) and *Child Protection and Early Years Teachers* (Open University Press 1992).

Erica De'Ath is Director of the National Stepfamily Association. She has written widely on parent education and support for families, particularly families experiencing change through separation, divorce, remarriage and repartnering. Previously Chief Executive of the Foundation for the Study of Infant Deaths, she has also worked at The Children's Society, and the National Children's Bureau, where she now serves as a member of the Board of Management.

Christine Harrison worked as a district team social worker and guardian ad litem before moving to a teaching post at Warwick University. Her main teaching and research interests are in the field of child protection, theories of child abuse and the development of law, policy and anti-oppressive practice.

Elaine Herbert is Deputy Head of Solihull's Preschool and Home Teaching Service. She works alongside parents and their preschool children in the home setting and believes strongly in the Warnock philosophy of 'parents as first educators' of young children. She is currently engaged in research for a higher degree in Early Years Education at the University of Warwick, looking more closely at the responses and reactions of fathers to the birth of a child with special needs.

Sonia Jackson, after many years lecturing in Social Work at Bristol

University, is now Professor of Applied Social Studies at University College, Swansea. She is currently working on a Department of Health-sponsored scheme to improve the quality of care for children 'looked after' by local authorities, and especially their educational opportunities. Her other interest is daycare. Her latest book, co-authored with Elinor Goldschmied, is *People Under Three: Young Children and Day Care*, also published by Routledge. Before coming into social work she was a psychologist and teacher, and she has shared in the upbringing of six children.

Cathy Nutbrown is Coordinator for Early Childhood Education with Sheffield Education Department. She has experience in early childhood education as a teacher and as a researcher, and is currently Vice-chair of OMEP(UK). She runs multi-disciplinary training courses on current issues affecting early childhood education, including work with parents, aspects of learning and development, and she has a special interest in children's learning patterns and their early literacy development.

Ann Sharp has taught nursery, infant and junior children, and she was in teacher education for five years before co-directing the Schools Council Project on Structuring Play in the Infant and First School. She was Nursery/Infant Adviser for Early Childhood Education in Sheffield for twelve years, a member of the Rumbold Committee of Inquiry into the Education of Children aged three to five, and the SEAC Task Group on Assessment at Key Stage 1. She has been involved in working with social services and education in the integration of under-fives' services and with the implementation of the Children Act 1989. Her involvement at national level in NAEIAC has enabled her to promote the needs of early childhood education, and she has recently completed the OFSTED training for inspection.

Judy Warner has worked in a variety of settings with young children, including a special school, nursery classes, a day nursery, a children's hospital and a college nursery. She was a local authority Day Care Adviser for many years, and has just taken up a new appointment as a Development Officer for the National Childminding Association.

Margy Whalley is head of Pen Green Centre in Corby. She has had experience of work with young children in South America and Papua New Guinea, and she is absorbed by community education and action, believing that 'Parents (principally women) and children are...undervalued and often feel powerless. Working collectively there is nothing that they cannot achieve.'

Vivienne Whittingham has degrees in sociology and social policy. She has a long experience of working with and for children, particularly the under-fives. After teaching in Ethiopia and England, she has worked with voluntary organisations at local and national levels; been involved in several childcare projects in the community; and is particularly interested in the needs of children of mixed parentage. She is married with two children.

Preface and acknowledgements

Working Together for Young Children is the product of many stimulating and enjoyable encounters and experiences over a number of years. Multi-professional work with young children and their families is a central tenet of the Children Act 1989, but effective collaboration and cooperation cannot be achieved without a clear understanding of one's own role and that of other voluntary and professional workers with whom one may come into contact. Additionally, a deep appreciation of life in families and the effects of contextual factors is essential to anyone striving for competence and confidence in their role, essential attributes without which workers may retreat behind a closed and authoritarian facade, so failing to act with empathy and dignity.

As editor, my first debt of gratitude is to all the contributors who have provided a broad spectrum of ideas and experiences; secondly, I would like to thank all the secretaries who helped them, and those in the Education Department at Warwick University, Sandra Dowse, Mary Graham and Margaret Handy, who have slaved over their word-processors; thanks also to colleagues, students and friends who have read, commented on, and discussed different parts of the book and/or the ideas presented; the attention, support and advice of Mari Shullaw and the staff at Routledge has been, without exception, caring and professional. Finally, as ever, I am personally in debt to my own family – Roy, Sacha and Ceris, (and Twiggy and Grips!) – for helping me remain human.

Introduction

This book is an attempt to explore some of the features of the lives of young children under five years of age, and of their families, in the UK in the 1990s, in the wake of the Children Act 1989. The basic, underpinning principles of this Act, which came into force on 14 October 1991, include:

(a) the child's interests are to be paramount, the child's voice heard, and the child's background (linguistic, cultural, religious, 'racial', etc.), gender, age or special need is to be taken into account;
(b) services, both statutory and voluntary, are to support families, which are believed, in the UK, to be the best context for children's upbringing;
(c) a new legal concept of parental responsibility is established; and
(d) the different agencies within local authorities and the community and voluntary organisations, must work together to provide effective services for children and their families.

The Act makes legal history in that this is the first piece of legislation to draw attention to the *duties* of parents, rather than simply reinforcing their rights over their children. Thus, together with other aspects relating to the recognition of children as people, the Act could be seen as an important lever for those advocating improvements in early childhood services, and for those who for many years have felt discouraged in their efforts at interdepartmental, or cross-agency, collaboration.

To expect effective collaboration between services to occur overnight would be naive. Each service, whether statutory or voluntary, has its own history and structure. Not only is it difficult for workers from one sector fully to appreciate the roles and procedures of colleagues from another, including the ways in which identities and philosophies are affected by training, status and conditions of employment, but there are currently the added confusions arising from massive upheavals in every single area, as a result of governmental reforms. This means that many workers are themselves unsure of their newly delineated role, and need time to come to terms with the changes and to explore the meaning of the new prescriptions in relation to their own personal beliefs about their professional identities. At the same time, some critics are concerned that while the Children Act's principles are noble, the new legislation is 'collusive in the support of a system that requires fundamental change' (Jones, 1994); and others argue that the reforms bear the hallmark of the New Right, and their expectation that citizens and their offspring will not be a drain on state resources, so that in spite of recent criticisms of social workers – and I would extend that to all the 'caring professions' – professionals are expected to 'delineate the boundaries between the public and the private, the state and the family'; and professional judgements become 'central in constituting the nature of "normal" family relations' (Parton 1991).

However, during the last thirty years there has been increasing recognition that children's development, while having certain universal, biologically predetermined parameters, is greatly influenced by context. For example, while four-month-old babies around the world seem to be programmed to smile at all comers as part of their survival mechanisms, the ways in which adults and older children respond to this depends upon social norms in that society, so that from a very early age individual children are part of a particular culture in which and through which they learn. As Woodhead et al. point out, 'children's welfare and development depends on their relationships with others' (1991: 3).

Some of the most influential child development theorists during the last three decades have been Bruner, Vygotsky, Bronfenbrenner and Donaldson, and perhaps the most important messages their work conveys to us are concerned with: the active nature of children's learning and their striving to make sense of whatever situation confronts them; the social, 'polyadic' (Schaffer 1984) or multi-personed, world in which they grow and learn; the ways in which aspects of society with which a child may not be in direct contact may nevertheless have a profound effect upon that child's upbringing and attitudes – for example, parental unemployment/ employment and conditions of service; a racist or anti-feminist ideology, and so on.

In particular, a society's concept, or concepts, of early childhood, the dominant ideas informing policies about what is appropriate provision for young children, where they should be, doing what and with whom, at certain ages, result in the availability – or not – of services which reflect the relative importance of a society's youngest members and those closest to them.

The current epidemic of reforms, the results of government policies based on their party philosophy of 'the market', have created an unfamiliar climate for workers in public services, who are unused to the cut and thrust of the business world, and competing to survive. Experienced professionals from different services argue that they are not only constrained by cutbacks in funding, but that the marketing model makes them feel ill at ease, deflected from what they perceive as their central role, and aware of potential, grave inequalities in the system. How effective can such reforms, implemented by anxious and disempowered workers, be in the long run?

In some areas of England and Wales the Children Act has been welcomed and multi-agency training undertaken. In others there are still pockets of doubt, and feelings of having too many pieces of legislation causing enormous upheavals to cope with at one time. For example, teachers trying to read, digest and implement all the material they have received concerning the 1988 Education Reform Act have found this alone burdensome, so it is hardly surprising they have had little time to consider the Children Act. Further, there are added confusions from the fact that the intentions of many of the pieces of education legislation, including the 1993 Bill currently passing through Parliament, appear to contradict the intentions of the Children Act.

Although many of the authors who have contributed chapters here find difficulties posed by legislative changes and the current economic climate, they recognise the overwhelming need for statutory and voluntary workers to maintain and develop positive attitudes towards supporting young children and their families, and to working together.

In her book about working collaboratively for children, Gillian Pugh, head of the Early Childhood Unit of the National Children's Bureau, quoted some of the Bureau's statements of principle:

that young children are important in their own right, and as a resource for the future;

that young children are valued and their full development is possible only if they live in an environment which reflects and respects their individual identity, culture and heritage;

that parents are primarily responsible for nurturing and supporting the development of their children and that this important role should be more highly valued by society;

that central and local government have a duty, working in partnership with parents, to ensure that services and support are available for families; services that encourage children's cognitive, social, emotional and physical development; and meet parents' needs for support for themselves and day care for their children.

(Pugh 1992; NCB 1990: 1)

Pugh (1992) then commented that embedded in these statements are values and principles which permeated the papers in that publication. The same could be said of this book, and it is hoped that it will offer yet another perspective on the ways in which it is necessary for our society to hold the needs of children and their families as central to concerns about its well-being and its future.

The intention of this book then, is to offer brief accounts of some of the services provided in the UK for our youngest children, and the roles of those working in them. The original brainstorm of potential contents included children's librarian to television producer, and lawyer to tumble-tots coach, and while many other volunteers and professionals do have a role to play in some, if not all, children's lives, failure to include them here is not intended to indicate any lack of appreciation for their particular expertise. Readers interested in exploring the roles and responsibilities of some of those omitted here should see Solity and Bickler (1993).

This book is aimed at those already working in the different voluntary and statutory agencies, together with parents and carers. Students from a variety of backgrounds may also find it illuminating, particularly those involved in the exciting new multi-professional courses, where the aim is to encourage a greater degree of understanding and collaboration across services. Despite the uncertainty, this collection of contributed chapters is offered in a spirit of hope!

After an introductory chapter exploring some of the beliefs, functions, and research evidence about 'the family', the book is divided into three main parts, each having a broad central theme. The first part focuses on services directed at all children, or potentially of use to children from any family situation – assuming the services are offered in the area in which the family lives, and, if fee-paying, that the family can afford the service.

Clare Blackburn presents and reviews the work of the health visitor in the current climate of change; Judy Warner offers a comprehensive overview of childminding, including some important observations about training needs; Cathy Nutbrown provides some case studies of the work of the qualified nursery teacher, showing in particular how provision that is intended to offer children cognitive/educational benefits needs to be sensitively planned and evaluated – provision that is still fun, but allows for children to dare to make their own mistakes and choices, to dare to learn. Margaret Brown discusses the role of playgroups in diversified early childhood services, and the massive contribution made by the Preschool Playgroups Association; and finally in Part I, Vivienne Whittingham discusses the challenges faced by private providers, the hurdles they must confront before even starting up a group, and the efforts being made to maintain and improve quality.

Part II poses questions about the ways in which parents and service providers can ameliorate the situation for young children 'in need', whether that need may be short-term, or likely to last a lifetime. In the first chapter of Part II Elaine Herbert discusses evidence from families whose children were identified as having special needs, very soon after their birth. In her concluding remarks she offers pointers to the improvement of services to special families, and they are pointers we could all use to evaluate our own particular field. Erica De'Ath demonstrates the ways in which the needs of the children themselves can be forgotten during parental separation and divorce. We could ensure a less traumatic experience at this time, and in the years, and possible serial family settings, that follow. Christine Harrison and Norma Baldwin discuss the role of the social worker, the difficulties of dealing with varying definitions of the concept 'in need', especially in a climate in which the discourse has shifted towards one characterised by legalism. Sonia Jackson provides an account and an analysis of the ways in which philosophy, policy and practice relating to the placement of children into care has changed over the years. In particular, she draws attention to the effects of the Children Act, and to the evidence that work needs to be done to foster the educational achievements of children in care. In other words, collaboration between services has not been sufficiently well developed in this area. In the last chapter of Part II I present some of the ways in which early childhood services in 'educare' facilities can support children and their parents during times of stress, but I also question the perpetuation of the idea of 'rescue' which is embedded in policies which target services on particular families or communities.

The third and final part of the book brings together chapters illustrating the need for comprehensiveness, continuity and collaboration at different levels – in early childhood settings; in a local authority; in course development for those working in the field. The authors present the issues and implications arising from, firstly, ideas about practice and provision which is intended to foster children's learning. The first chapter, by Margy Whalley, offers insights into the developments needed in provision which has been labelled daycare, if all children are to be entitled to high-quality early learning experiences, whatever the type of service to which their families have access. Following this, Audrey Curtis explores recent training initiatives, at the same time questioning the wisdom of policies to change the level of education required of those who work with young children. The final chapter here, by Ann Sharp, provides an overview of the development of services in one local authority, an authority where the will to provide comprehensive, coordinated services is ever-present, but is hampered by other difficulties, especially finance. This is a fitting point at which to offer some final, concluding remarks, and these form my 'postscript' to the book.

REFERENCES

Jones, A. (1994) 'Anti-racist child protection', in T.David (ed.) *Working together to protect children: multiprofessionalism and the Children Act 1989.* Stoke-on-Trent, Trentham Books.

National Children's Bureau: Under Fives' Unit (1990) *A Policy for Young Children.* London, National Children's Bureau.

Parton, N. (1991) *Governing the Family.* London, Macmillan.

Pugh, G. (ed.) (1992) *Contemporary Issues in the Early Years: Working Collaboratively for Children.* London, National Children's Bureau/Paul Chapman.

Schaffer, H.R. (1984) *The Child's Entry into a Social World.* London, Academic Press.

Solity, J.E. and Bickler, G.J. (1993) *Support Services: Issues for Education, Health and Social Service Professionals*. London, Cassell.

Woodhead, M., Carr, R. and Light, P. (1991) *Becoming a Person*. London, Routledge/Open University.

Chapter 1

What's so special about families?

Tricia David

ENTERING THE WORLD, AND A FAMILY

I remember looking round the labour ward to see if there had been some mistake. I had been handed a beautiful baby who looked nothing like the one I had imagined during my pregnancy, but I was the only woman in there giving birth, so she must be 'mine'. As an ex-student of the Newsons, whose pioneering studies carried out in the 1960s (1965, 1968) provided a new kind of information about families, babyhood and early childhood, I should have been better prepared for this. Maybe we have come to rely too much on cognitive faculties based on 'scientific evidence' and not enough on the excitement, but also the acceptance, of nature's ability to startle us. Most of all, however we react, the memory of each childbirth is likely to be something we carry with us all our lives, in the most minute and vivid detail.

Understanding the biology of human reproduction is easy – it is comprehending the psychology of it that is difficult. Being able to appreciate and prepare for imminent childbirth is one thing; in the event, how you, your partner or any other member of the family reacts – especially the newborn – can be surprising, and sometimes confusing.

Very often people use the term family when they mean household. Family is perhaps more problematic. Where does one draw the line? When does one become a 'new' family, and does one remain part of older, extended family networks, when one settles down with a partner perhaps? Certainly most children include people not related to them by blood, and people who no longer live with them, in their drawings of their families, and they will often also include their pets. Perhaps as far as children are concerned it is their perception of the importance of a particular relationship that causes them to include someone in their depictions of their family. In this book the word parent has been used to represent the person or persons taking parental responsibility for the child. In some cases this will indeed be their 'natural parent', in others it will not, but the bonds are assumed, nevertheless to be as 'hot' and the emotional investment no less strong. This chapter explores functions of the family, the roles of some of its members in relation to their experiences with a baby or young child, and some of the research information which those in the 'caring professions' can draw upon to develop their work.

THE FAMILY

The stereotyped notion of 'the family', two married parents of the opposite sex, with two children and only the father's income, is a reality for only one family in seven today (Roll 1991). Furthermore, there is evidence (Graham 1984) indicating that single parenthood and divorce are not the modern phenomena they have been painted, and that in Victorian times illegitimate births were at a higher rate than in the mid- twentieth century, and that one in three of the marriages of the 1860s would have ended within twenty years, usually as a result of the death of one partner. This means that family diversity is not new, and the designation of 1994 as 'International Year of the Family' by the UN seems unfortunate – perhaps 'Families Year' might have been more appropriate.

FUNCTIONS OF FAMILIES

Abbott (1989) suggests that the historical evidence we have indicates that in the past children would have lived in varied forms of the family, and that these would have included relatives and friends from a wider kinship group than is usually so today. Further, according to anthropologists, there is no evidence that the family as we know it is a 'natural' phenomenon. Mitterauer and Sieder (1982) argue that the patriarchal model of the family, which included safety-nets for the aged, infirm or other dependent kin, was far more a feature of life in other European countries than of Britain, perhaps because the industrial revolution affected life in this country earlier. Further, Dahlstrom's (1989) research indicates that despite anxieties about the destruction of the family, it is the forms rather than the functions of families that have changed. These functions have been as follows, and while these prevail to some extent, the state or other bodies have taken over some of the responsibilities, or they have been modified. The *reproductive* function has been considerably modified in today's families, and no longer forms a basic *raison d'être* of family life. In the past, childbirth was generally the accepted fate of married women, unless infertility prevented conception. In today's society, women are perceived as having much greater choice about motherhood, and certainly about the number of children they bear. The statistics (Coote *et al.* 1990) indicate that many younger women are leaving their first pregnancy until later in life, that many more than a generation ago choose to remain unmarried to their partner or to become a single parent, and that the average number of offspring, at less than two per woman, means those currently in the childbearing age-range are not replacing themselves. The subsequent demographic changes are therefore destined to have severe repercussions over the next twenty to thirty years, with a relatively small number of young workers supporting a large cohort of elderly – some of whom will not be fit to continue in employment, even if this were possible.

Other functions of the family would have included: the *religious*, Mitterauer and Sieder (1982) argue that religion would have originally meant ancestor-worship, and the family was seen as having responsibility for the induction of the young into this belief system, so ensuring powerful control remained in the hands of the most senior member/s of the family, but this function was over-taken by community and church long ago; a *judicial* function, for example, in some societies, the family would be expected to take the law into its own hands and seek revenge for a wrong, and we can still see this in action through both legal and other channels; a protective function, for example, a wife, children and servants would have come under the protection of their master; an economic function, families supported children, the sick, elderly, and so on, who were unproductive; a *socialising* function, babies and children would be cared for and taught (i.e. educated as we know this, or a craft or trade), and inducted into wider society by the family; and, finally, a *cultural* function.

Much of today's debate about the family is actually concerned with the balance between family and state responsibilities. How should policies be formulated to take account of the rights of the individual within the family? For we cannot assume that leaving families alone will mean each member gets a fair deal.

Ideas about the upbringing of boys and girls still hold sway that have their roots in the long-lost division of labour between husband and wife....Such a cultural lag is often to be noted in the history of the family because of its inherent conservatism.

(Mitterauer and Sieder 1982: 90)

The effects of outmoded differences in status can be seen in Hilary Graham's (1984) research evidence on the distribution of food and income, for example, within families, with women and children, particularly those living in poverty, still conceding precedence to adult males. Some feminist theorists (e.g. Barrett and McIntosh 1982) argue that the nuclear family is the site of oppression for women and children and they are thus concerned about the extent of the ideological influence of the concept of 'the family'. However, they also argue that although it remains ideologically powerful, this concept is not translated into reality in the way in which most people live their lives today.

Recognising the influence of this ideology, however, in exploring the inequalities experienced by women and children can help one understand why being a single mother actually makes more sense if one lives 'on the breadline'. For example, one then has greater control of one's income, and the freedom to use it to the benefit of one's children. To quote one single mother: 'Some unemployed men end up behaving like spoilt and selfish children – you can do without the aggro, and it's one less "child" to look after.' We need to develop the education of young people, in particular challenging attitudes about gender and power, if we are to change the ways boys and young men are socialized (Harrison 1993).

LIFE IN A FAMILY

What do we know about the relationships formed by babies and young children with their mothers, their fathers, siblings, grandparents, other home-based carers and friends?

Much of the early research into the development of babies and young children focused almost exclusively on the mother–child bond and relationship (e.g. Bowlby 1953; Winnicott 1964). Woollett and Phoenix, who together with Lloyd have gathered a set of papers which challenge the dominant discourses about motherhood, argue that

> developmental psychologists employ theoretical models which are reliant on models of monotropic or exclusive existence. This has implications for how mothers experience the upbringing of two children but also for how they experience motherhood as their children grow up. Older children tend to be less extensively studied.
>
> (Woollett and Phoenix 1991: 222)

Further, Woollett and Phoenix (1991) discuss the reluctance of psychologists to recognise that women's experience and ideas of motherhood are variable, and that those who suggest motherhood as offering unique opportunities for adult development equate motherhood with adult status for females, thus failing to acknowledge women's other achievements and contributions. Such eulogising about the 'joys of motherhood' provides a false representation.

On the other hand, they continue. Some feminist literature has been overly negative in its portrayal of motherhood and oppression, and neither offers a way forward which is realistic about both joys and difficulties. Moss (1990) has argued we need national policies similar to those which were, until the recent change of government, prevalent in Sweden, where the whole of society is seen as responsible for its children. It seems likely that until we do have commitment of this kind, the needs and rights of women and their children will be seen as contradicting each other. We have known for some time that a considerable number of young mothers suffer from depression (Brown and Harris 1978), and this must not only be damaging to themselves, but hardly conducive to an environment in which young children will be likely to experience appropriate stimulation and role modelling. We need to expose the ecological system producing such conditions. Professionals and volunteers could try making use of the Children Act 1989 to press for greater support for mothers and children.

In the meantime, whether from real choice or from necessity/social pressure, most mothers will indeed be the main carers of their children in the first months and years of life. Although some researchers continue to seek evidence about the negative effects of 'other care' (e.g. Belsky 1988), the debate has moved on as far as those who are convinced that it is the quality, not the fact, of non-maternal/own family experience that is important in the earliest years.

We know from studies of children raised on kibbutzim that despite spending a greater proportion of the day with their metapulets (nurses), children formed their strongest bonds with their own parents. In another study, Webb (1984) explored the relationships of children under five who had experienced multiple caring as a result of parental employment, in the USA. She found that children who were positive and well able to cope with their lives had formed strong attachments to their parents, and that such parents used strategies Webb called 'bugging and nudging'(i.e. encouraging, showing what you do matters and is important); engage in special family rituals, idiosyncratic behaviour which is meaningful to that family; and use pet names. These indicators seem to point to the quality of the adult–child relationships – firstly, the ways in which the children are recognised as people with an understanding of, and the possibility of changing or introducing, rituals etc.; secondly, commitment, especially the commitment to time to engage in these interactions; and thirdly, constancy.

The role of fathers has received the attention of researchers (e.g. Lamb 1981; Lewis 1986), particularly during the last ten to fifteen years. However, as Elaine Herbert's new research (see Chapter 7) is demonstrating, only certain fathers have been included in these studies, so, like the stereotyped image of motherhood, it may be that what we know about fatherhood comes largely from a white, middle-class, employed, professional group.

White and Woollett (1991), for example, criticise research so far because it portrays the overall roles of fathers as similar to that of mothers, and focuses too narrowly on what fathers do, rather than the frequency or style in which they do it. What may be more important is their sensitivity (or not) to their child during such interactions. They cite the example of rough-and-tumble play, saying that a father who engages in this on the child's initiative, and who is responsive to the child's behaviours will be evoking different consequences for that child from those of a father who is only aware of his own actions and intentions.

In addition to fatherhood being about interactions with children, it is also about role modelling and the ways in which children learn from their perceptions of the relationship between their parents, and between their parents and other family members. Although some surveys indicate that fathers believe they are 'new men' (Dex 1985), other studies show that fathers tend, on the whole, to choose which tasks they will undertake, and that their levels of engagement are not as high as they think (Brannen and Moss 1991). To be fair, those fathers who are employed are unlikely to have a great many opportunities to do as much as they might like, since over 80 per cent of fathers of children aged 0–4 spend over forty hours per week at work (Cohen and Fraser 1991). In other words, in families where there are two parents, roles are often delineated in traditional ways, thus working mothers, even when they have a partner, are still likely to be overburdened and in need of support.

It is also interesting to note the ways in which young children themselves conceptualise the role of the father. Even children from families where both parents go out to work, and some where only the mother does so, will play in the home corner of a nursery or infant classroom according to very stereotyped conventions. Boys assigned the role of father tend to sit to be waited on at table (for breakfast), then to leave, saying they are going to work, only to lurk round the corner for a few minutes until returning with 'I'm home!'. What actually happens during the supposed work session is rarely discussed or portrayed in the dramatic play. Further, when boys alone take over the home corner, they are likely to convert it into something else – say, a ship or a kennel.

When John, aged four, was alone in the home corner he suddenly began swirling the plastic and metal cups, saucers, plates and teapot around in the 'sink' with such ferocity the clatter was tremendous. Sally, the nursery nurse, went to ask him what was happening, to which he replied 'My wife's left and I've got to do all this myself.'

One cannot help feeling that a text such as 'Families without fatherhood' (Dennis and Erdos 1992) reinforces the old stereotypes of the father as strong breadwinner and disciplinarian – master of the house – despite providing some powerful evidence about the way children are generally more able to thrive in families with a stable father-figure. The book accuses left-wing intellectuals of providing a rationale for men's absence, instead of exploring the fact that unless society provides young males with other than economic roles in family life, they will have no way of knowing how to function well in relation to a partner and/or children in the event of unemployment. Measures such as the introduction of the Child Support Agency and the new laws governing benefit payments to single mothers do appear to be based on a notion of forcing a father to stay in a family, or a woman to retain a partner, because they would otherwise lack the necessary funds to survive, rather than because they are a group of people who choose to live together for mutual support and enjoyment of each other's company.

Other members of the nuclear and extended family are being increasingly shown to hold great importance to young children, for example, in Dunn and Kendrick's work on siblings (1982), Rubin's (1980) on friends and peer-relations, Webb (1984) on a range of teenage and adult 'babysitters', Cunningham-Burley (1987) on grandparenting. A significant ten-year study by Cochran et al. (1990), concerned with the social networks of parents and children and using an ecological systems approach, draws attention to the ways in which children form meaningful relationships, and develop cognitively, during shared tasks with interested adults, the best results being obtained when those adults were members of the child's own family. For example, the reading scores of boys seemed to be related to whether or not their fathers engaged in activities with them, even when compared with a group who had the same number of adult contacts; for boys with no father-figure at home, another adult male, regarded by the child as a member of the family, would produce the same effect. For children from single-parent families, achievement at school correlated with the number of adult relatives who took the child on outings, etc.

Cochran et al. (1990) argue therefore, that families, given stress-free conditions in which they can function adequately, are capable of fulfilling the basic developmental needs of their members, whether adults or children. However, they fear that when levels of stress become intolerable, individual family members may resort to survival behaviours which are actually counter to the interests of the weakest members, and which curtail their capacity to interact in the service of each other.

OTHER CARE

One of the functions of the family which it is particularly pertinent to consider in the current context is that of early care and education. Gillian Pugh has produced much evidence and many statements (e.g. 1992, 1992a) arguing for comprehensive, high-quality services for young children and their parents. Education and care facilities are considered in Parts II and III of the book. However, for children under five whose parents (i.e. mothers) wish to, or have to, go out to work, the record of the UK is very dismal compared with our European partner countries. Some of the arguments presented in this country include ideas about the family and early socialisation, despite the fact that research (e.g. Speekman Klass 1986) indicates that group provision does not hinder the development of the autonomous individual. Other arguments posed against wider service provision and central government intervention range around suspected ill effects on children, and costs to the public purse.

In the Scandinavian countries, where childcare provision has been more plentiful than in Britain (Vilien, 1993), and where young children may spend long hours in care facilities while parents are employed, there is some anxiety about the possibility of discontinuity for children living in two very different and distinct settings. However, research from Sweden (Hwang *et al.* 1991) indicates that as long as the quality of the provision is high, the effects on children are positive, and it is the quality of home life which will result in positive or negative outcomes in later academic performance.

As for the cost argument, studies by Cohen and Fraser (1991) and by Holtermann (1992) have demonstrated that the flow-back to the public purse from taxation of women's earnings would more than repay any investment in high quality services.

CONCLUSIONS

In 'Parenting: A job for life' Pugh *et al.* (1982) discuss the ways in which families grow and change. They are not static, but dynamic, organic structures which can be at one and the same time the source of positive and negative experiences for members. Like the children in them (if there are any), the adults too grow and change, and while some new members arrive, through partnership, marriage or birth, others are lost through departures, removals or deaths.

How a society responds to the changing needs of its members, especially those who are the most vulnerable, must surely be a mark of its level of civilisation. How workers are enabled to empower families, to work in partnership with them (Pugh and De'Ath 1989), to cater flexibly for what the families themselves identify as their needs seems to be the challenge for professional and voluntary agency managers for the 1990s.

REFERENCES

Abbott, P. (1989) 'Family lifestyles and structures', in W. Stainton Rogers, D. Hevey and E. Ash (eds) *Child Abuse and Neglect*. London, Batsford/Open University.

Barrett, M. and McIntosh, M. (1982) *The Anti-social Family*. London, Verso/NLB.

Belsky, J. (1988) 'The "effects" of infant daycare reconsidered', *Early Childhood Research Quarterly*, 3, 235–72.

Bowlby, J. (1953) *Child Care and the Growth of Love*. Harmondsworth, Penguin.

Brannen, J. and Moss, P. (1991) *Managing Mothers*. London, Unwin Hyman.

Brown, G. and Harris, T.D. (1978) *Social Origins of Depression*. London, Tavistock.

Cochran, M., Larner, M., Riley, D., Gunnarsson, L. and Hendreson, C.R. (1990) *Extending Families*. Cambridge, Cambridge University Press.

Cohen, B. and Fraser, N. (1991) *Childcare in a Modern Welfare System*. London, IPPR.

Coote, A., Hartman, H. and Hewitt, P. (1990) *The Family Way, a New Approach to Policy-making*. London, IPPR.

Cunningham-Burley, S. (1987) 'The experience of grandfatherhood', in C.Lewis and M.O'Brien (eds) *Reassessing Fatherhood*. London, Sage.

Dahlstrom, E. (1989) 'Theories and ideology of family function, gender relations and human reproduction', in K.Boh, M.Bak, C.Clason, M.Pankratova, J.Qvortup, B.G.Sgritta and K.Aerness (eds) *Changing patterns of European Family Life*. London, Routledge.

Dennis, N. and Erdos, G. (1992) *Families without Fatherhood*. London, IEA Health and Welfare Unit.

Dex, S. (1985) *The Sexual Division of Work*. Brighton, Wheatsheaf.

Dunn, J. and Kendrick, C. (1982) *Siblings: Love, Envy and Understanding*. Cambridge, MA, Harvard University Press.

Graham, H. (1984) *Women, Health and the Family*. Brighton, Wheatsheaf.

Harrison, C. (1993) 'Young men, power and sexuality', paper presented at the 4th ISPCAN European Conference on Child Abuse and Neglect, Abano Terme, Padova, Italy, March 1993.

Holtermann, S. (1992) *Investing in Young Children: Costing an Education and Daycare Service*. London, National Children's Bureau.

Hwang, C.P., Broberg, A. and Lamb, M.E. (1991) 'Swedish childcare research', in P. Moss and E. Melhuish (eds) *Day Care for Young Children. International Perspectives*. London, Routledge.

Lamb, M.E. (1981) *The Role of the Father in Child Development*. New York, Wiley.

Lewis, C. (1986) *Becoming a Father*. Milton Keynes, Open University Press.

Mitterauer, M. and Sieder, R. (1982) *The European Family*. Oxford, Basil Blackwell.

Moss, P. (1990) 'Work, family and the care of children: equality and responsibility', *Children and Society*, 4, 2, 145–66.

Newson, J. and Newson, E. (1965) *Patterns of Infant Care*. Harmondsworth, Penguin.

—— (1968) *Four Years Old in an Urban Community*. Harmondsworth, Penguin.

Pugh, G. (1992) (ed.) *Contemporary Issues in the Early Years*. London, National Children's Bureau/Paul Chapman.

—— (1992a) *An equal start for all our children?*. London, TES/Greenwich.

Pugh, G. and De'Ath, E. (1989) *Working Towards Partnership in the Early Years*. London, National Children's Bureau.

Pugh, G., Torkington, K. and Kidd, J. (1982) *A Job for Life*. London, National Children's Bureau.

Roll, J. (1991) *What is a Family?*. London, FPSC.

Rubin, Z. (1980) *Children's Friendships*. Cambridge, MA, ABT Associates.

Speekman Klass, C. (1986) *The Autonomous Child*. London, Falmer Press.

Vilien, K. (1993) 'Provision for preschool children in Denmark. In T.David (ed.) *Educating our Youngest Children: European Perspectives*. London, Paul Chapman.

Webb, N.B. (1984) *Preschool Children with Working Parents: an analysis of attachment*. New York, University Press of America.

White, D.G. and Woollett, E.A. (1991) 'The father's role in the neo-natal period', in M.Woodhead, R.Carr and P.Light (eds) *Becoming a Person*. London, Routledge /Open University.

Winnicott, D.W. (1964) *The Child, the Family and the Outside World*. Harmondsworth, Penguin.

Woollett, A. and Phoenix, A. (1991) 'Afterword: issues related to motherhood', in A.Phoenix, A.Woollett and E.Lloyd (eds) *Motherhood: Meanings, Practices and Ideologies*. London, Sage.

Part I

Services for young children and their families

Chapter 2

In sickness and in health

Clare Blackburn

INTRODUCTION

Caring for young children in sickness and in health involves meeting and dealing with a wide range of health care professionals. For many people, early parenthood is the first time they have had any extensive contact with health care practitioners. It is hardly surprising then, that many of the difficulties associated with caring for young children are compounded by the confusion parents experience when they come into contact with an array of health care practitioners. Parents are not the only ones who are confused about the roles and responsibilities of health care practitioners. Practitioners from other statutory and voluntary sectors also find it difficult to establish what various groups of health care practitioners do and how they relate to families. As a result, collaborative work has suffered and is often infused with tensions concerning who should be doing what in relation to family care.

This chapter will discuss the roles and responsibilities of health visitors, a group of health care practitioners with whom families commonly come into contact. It examines the way in which they relate to families as family support workers and as public health workers. It begins with a discussion of how legislation and government initiatives are restructuring the health services and reshaping the services that health visitors are able to offer.

HEALTH SERVICES IN THE 1990s

Health visiting services are provided within a turbulent and constantly changing health service. They currently have to respond to changing health needs which stem from the success of preventive health measures, advances in medical treatment, and social, economic and demographic changes which have created new and varied health needs. Attempts to respond to and meet new health needs have been accompanied by new legislation and government initiatives which together amount to a fundamental reorganisation of health service provision. These changes have affected the roles and responsibilities of all health service workers, particularly health visitors. Understanding the latters' role and responsibilities then, is dependent on an understanding of the organisation of the health services in the 1990s.

The National Health Service and Community Care Act 1990 (House of Commons 1990) has brought about significant changes in provision. This Act has essentially introduced a market economy into the arena of health care as a way of bringing about cost improvements in the National Health Service (NHS). Its emphasis on effectiveness, efficiency and quality control has introduced different models of health care from those with which we are familiar. The most obvious feature has been the separation of purchaser-provider functions. Prior to implementation of the Act, purchaser-provider functions in the state sector were not seen as separate. District Health Authorities (DHAs) were seen as responsible for both functions: deciding on what health services should be provided and for providing them, budgets permitting. DHAs are now charged with the responsibility to purchase services on behalf of the local population, according to local need. The Act allows organisations and units, some of which may be DHA-managed, to become autonomous providers of services.

Today's health service is an internal market where health care is available from a variety of providers. It is a market where providers of services (self-governing hospitals and NHS Trusts, DHA-managed units and private and voluntary organisations) can sell their services to purchasers (District Health Authorities, GP fund-holders, other NHS Trusts and private and voluntary organisations).

The introduction of the National Health Service and Community Care Act has been accompanied by the establishment of a new general practitioner contract. This contract emerged following protracted negotiations on the implementation of the 1989 White Paper *Promoting Better Health* (Department of Health 1989), which was concerned with primary health care. The new contract paved the way for a general practitioner fund-holding scheme. This scheme gives practices the option to control their own budgets or to allow them to continue under a scheme where the budget is managed by the Family Health Service Authority.

Fund-holding practices are expected to contract with hospitals for certain services and to provide a full range of primary health care services (non-hospital health care services) for their patients. As a result, many services previously provided by community units of DHAs, for example, child health clinics and family planning services, are (or should be) provided by fund-holding general practices for their own patients. Families not registered with a fund-holding practice can still use existing DHA-provided primary care services – although there is evidence to suggest that they are in decline (Potrykus 1992) – or the services provided by their own general practitioner, if they exist.

HEALTH VISITORS

Together, the changes stemming from the National Health Service and Community Care Act and the new general practitioner contract have resulted in health care provision becoming increasingly complex and fragmented. The shape of health visiting work is in constant flux. It not only depends on what the health visiting profession currently perceives its role and function to be, but also on what services purchasers wish to buy and on what provision employers see as important to offer.

Reorganisation of the NHS has resulted in health visitors being employed by a diversity of provider units. Some work for NHS Trusts, while others work for directly managed DHA units, depending on the local situation. Each unit, whether a Trust or a directly managed unit, may have its own philosophy or mission statement to guide service provision, including health visiting provision for families. Although fund-holding practices are not able to employ health visitors directly (at least not yet), since 1993 they have been able to buy in health visiting services from NHS Trusts or health authority managed community health units, inevitably shaping health visiting work in a locality.

While it is difficult to define clearly the current roles and responsibilities of health visitors, it is possible to describe some common features that underpin health visiting work, giving it some unifying threads. The key to all health visiting work is that, unlike other areas of community nursing (with the exception of school nursing), it is predominantly concerned with the well population. Health visitors' prime concern is promoting health and preventing physical, mental and social ill health. Health is seen as something that cannot be separated from its social and economic context. Health visiting work then, is concerned not only with health behaviour but also with the social and material circumstances that shape that behaviour and create family health needs.

Promoting health and preventing disease requires a diversity and breadth of skills. Health visitors are registered (trained) nurses and some are also trained midwives. They often have many years of experience of work in the hospital sector. To prepare them for working in a community health setting, they have all successfully completed a one-year health visiting course in an institute of higher education to enable them to redirect their nursing skills towards the preventive, rather than curative, aspects of health work.

A NEEDS-RELATED APPROACH

A needs-related approach is a core feature of health visiting work. This stems from the recognition that practice must be directly related to the needs of the population being served (Health Visitors' Association 1992). This approach rests on the search for and identification of health needs and has been a feature of health visiting since its inception.

Identifying health needs at the level of the family has been the most common aspect of this work. Most health visitors try to meet expectant parents during the antenatal period to build up a relationship prior to the birth of a child and to identify with parents any immediate and potential health needs that are likely to be relevant following the birth. They commonly take over from midwives around the eleventh day after the birth of a child (although this may be later if a midwife is still visiting), to begin the task of enabling parents to identify their immediate and long-term health needs: their need for support, information, skills and access to health and social care provision. Using assessment procedures, health visitors also try to identify health needs and problems that may not be immediately apparent, for example, developmental delay, the early signs of a disease or conditions such as poor hearing and speech, so that families can be referred to appropriate services at an early stage. All health visitors are experts in child health and are trained to carry out child health surveillance programmes.

Identifying health needs at community level has only recently become a core component of health visiting practice. Recognising that many individual and family health needs can only be met by community provision has led the way to community health needs assessment exercises. The identification of community health needs has further been driven by two additional factors: the new requirement for directors of public health to provide a report on the state of public health of the local population, and the responsibility placed on DHAs to purchase services to meet local health needs.

Health visitors, with their unique and extensive knowledge of local populations, and up-to-date data bases of family health records, provide a 'live register of people on the ground' (Goodwin 1992). With this knowledge and bank of data, they are able to identify everyday health experiences and needs that cannot easily or accurately be identified through the top–down health needs assessment exercises currently carried out by many public health departments. The search for and identification of community health needs is carried out through what health visitors commonly call 'health profiling'. Health profiles contain data on the health status and health experiences of the local population, for example, on immunisation take-up rates, child accident rates, illnesses common in the locality and in some cases, local people's experiences of using local health services. They also contain data on the social and economic context within which health is experienced; thus health profiles are likely to contain useful information on local housing circumstances, unemployment levels, environmental hazards, social support networks and the availability of health and welfare provision. Health profiles are usually compiled for general practice populations or small geographical areas, depending on whether health visitors are geographically based or based in general practices.

Identifying health needs remains predominantly a professional activity. The recognition that services should be based on client-identified need (needs that are felt and expressed by individuals, groups and communities), rather than solely on needs identified by professionals, has led some health visitors to think about how they can share health profiling activities with local people and other local practitioners, for example, social workers and community workers. In some areas, joint health profiles have been successfully compiled with health visitors working in partnership with local people and other locality workers (O'Gorman and Moore 1990).

The information from health visitors' health profiles is being used for several purposes. Where health profiling activities have been effectively implemented, they are being used to drive the purchaser-provider contracting process so that primary care services can be purchased to meet the needs of local services. Health profile information is also likely to be useful to local authorities, who are required, under The Children Act, to provide services for children in need and their families. Health profile information is also increasingly being used by health visitors themselves and their managers as a basis for prioritising, planning, implementing and evaluating practice. It is used to inform two core areas of health visiting work: family health promotion work and public health work.

FAMILY HEALTH PROMOTION WORK

Many health visitors currently spend much of their time on family health promotion work. While health visiting work is not limited to working with families with young children – many health visitors also work with adult groups and groups with special needs, for example, homeless people and people with AIDS – most of the work is concerned with caring for families with young children. Early parenthood and childhood are perceived as periods when families need increased support and times for promoting health and preventing disease.

A needs-based approach is moving health visiting away from routine visiting to all families, following a prescribed menu of care for all, to one that attempts to respond to the specific health needs of individual families. This has widened the debate concerning whether health visiting should be a universal or a selective service. Traditionally, health visitors have offered, in theory at least, a routine menu of care and a standard home visiting and clinic appointment programme to all families, regardless of whether families felt they needed it. While visiting at non-crisis times is seen as central to any preventive programme of health care, it is felt that a needs-based approach means that contracts should be negotiated. The trend now appears to be towards offering a service that is open to all families, and a programme of contacts that reflects the needs and wishes of individual families. This allows health visitors to offer a selective service to groups with additional or special needs alongside, for example, families living in poor social and material conditions.

Rising poverty levels and deteriorating material circumstances in the UK have resulted in many families requiring help to avoid or cope with the worst aspects of poverty and material deprivation. Promoting health in poverty is now a key area of work for health visiting and there has been a growing recognition within the profession that practice must seek to address poverty as a major health factor (Blackburn 1991b). As a consequence, health visitors are providing increased support for low-income families, looking at ways in which they can assist families to maximise incomes through claiming benefits to which they are entitled, through welfare rights advice and community development work to improve local childcare resources and resources to support women (Brummell 1993).

Working in partnership with families is considered a core value of health visiting. Like other practitioner groups working with families with young children, the nature of the job means that health visitors tread a fine line between partnership and social policing. Criticisms of health visiting practice, together with the need to meet the requirements laid down by The Children Act, have led many health visitors to think about how they can enhance partnership styles of work. Working in partnership with families to construct health care plans has become increasingly common. Client-held records are another example of developments in this area. Using a nationally produced or a locally developed record card, families themselves, rather than health visitors or clinics, are able to hold a child's main health record where this system is in operation. Some health visitors still need to be convinced of the value of this system and it is likely to be some time before all areas move over to parent-held records.

There are times when health visitors, inevitably, move away from true partnership. Health visitors may decide to implement a programme of contact with a family, or a more intensive programme than one desired by a family, if they feel that a child is at risk, physically, mentally or socially. While health visiting does not see itself as a child protection agency in the same way as social work, its child health responsibilities inevitably pull it into this area of work. A growing concern expressed by health visitors is the shortage of social workers to carry out child protection work. In many areas, health visitors are left to monitor children at risk without social work support. This reduces health visiting resources to carry out health promotion work and can make it difficult, if not impossible, for them to work with a family on other issues important to health or to maintain a positive relationship with families after a child protection issue has been resolved.

Health visitors are the family health promotion specialists within the primary health care team. In addition to expertise in child health surveillance, health visitors are also able to offer counselling and advice on a wide range of health matters. Common areas of work with young families include counselling to increase take-up of immunisation and other preventive health services, such as hearing tests, cervical cytology, family planning services and coronary heart disease screening. They also have the expertise to help families to change aspects of health behaviour they wish to change, material and social circumstances permitting, including diet, smoking and exercise patterns. Parents also commonly use health visiting services for information and advice on the management of minor illness and accidents and on managing aspects of children's behaviour that families may find difficult, for example, disturbed sleep patterns, toilet training and bed-wetting.

Many parents, particularly mothers, use health visiting services for concerns relating to their own health. Health visitors commonly provide support for lonely, isolated and depressed mothers. As well as providing one-to-one support on issues relating to health, health visitors also see building up social support networks as important. Bringing women together for mutual support, through parent support groups and women's groups, has become a key feature of health visiting work.

Many family health needs cannot be met within the family or with the help of health visitors. Families frequently need to use services provided by other arms of the health service and by other agencies, including housing departments, social services, education departments, the Benefits Agency, voluntary sector agencies and leisure services. Providing information about and helping people to use these services is seen as essential. Many families, especially those living in poor material and social circumstances, find it difficult to negotiate access to services and social provision and need the support of health visitors to do so.

PUBLIC HEALTH WORK

In addition to health promotion work with individual families, health visitors are increasingly seeing themselves as public health workers, assisting communities to recognise and meet their collective health needs, including securing resources to do so. Addressing issues of inequalities in health are seen as central to this work. Community health profiles are increasingly being used to identify where multi-professional work and work with the community is needed. Although many health visitors have some way to go before they can accurately describe themselves as true public health workers, there are health visiting initiatives and projects that are good examples of work in this area.

Most common are community wide campaigns to increase awareness of specific health issues, for example, coronary health disease or child safety and campaigns to increase uptake of services, for example, immunisation services. Work with specific groups in the community, such as groups of unemployed people and youth groups, to raise awareness of health issues and health service provision is also not uncommon (Drennan 1986). Billingham's work (1989) with young mothers in Nottingham, using a group work approach to improve access to and uptake of health services, is a good example of this type of work.

Other work that can be broadly described as fitting into a public health brief includes collaboration with other workers to provide information and services for the community. Health visitors in Brent, for example, have worked with other practitioner groups to provide a range of services from a community flat on a housing estate, including setting up a a mental health support group, to a toy library and playgroup (Sachs 1990).

Other health visitors play an important role in the formation of, or representation of, special interest or pressure groups. Health visitors can, and do act as lobbyists on community issues by feeding information to managers, employers, other agencies and policy-makers. Representing parents' views, for example on lack of nursery provision, supported by health profile information, has served to protect services under threat. Supporting a parent group to lobby on its own behalf also appears to be a feature of their public health work. Health visiting support of a successful parents' campaign for safe play facilities on a council estate has been described and is not atypical of health visiting work in this area (Blackburn 1991a).

CONCLUSION

Health visitors are still developing many aspects of their role as family health promotion and public health promotion workers. Across the UK, the extent to which a needs-based approach and the concept of partnership are being utilised varies according to geographical area, and to health visiting teams within areas.

The turbulent state of the health service means that the roles and responsibilities of health visitors are currently in a state of flux. The degree to which family public health and public health promotion work remain core components of their work will depend, to a large extent, on health visitors' ability to show that this work is effective in bringing about health gain to families, and therefore, is worth purchasing from provider units. Health promotion is a fundamental part of the new health strategy for England, *The Health of the Nation*. As a strategy, it confirms the importance of health practitioner groups, like health visiting, who see health promotion as their primary concern. However, many health visitors fear that this strategy will pull them back into reactive styles of work, concerned with health screening and individual health behaviour change, and will limit the opportunities to carry out the broader health promotion work, particularly at the level of the community, that is currently a developing and dynamic response to family and community health needs.

REFERENCES

Billingham, K. (1989) '49 Cope Street: working in partnership with parents', *Health Visitor*, 62, 5, 156–7.
Blackburn, C. (1991a) 'The Boxhill parents' group', in Child Accident Prevention Trust, *Preventing Accidents to Children: A Training Resource for Health Visitors*. London, Health Education Authority.
Blackburn, C. (1991b) *Poverty and Health: Working with Families*. Milton Keynes, Open University Press.
Brummell, K. (1993) 'Practical ways of working with families in poverty', *Primary Health Care*, February.
Department of Health (1989) *Promoting Better Health*. London, HMSO.
Drennan, V. (1986) *Health Visitors and Groups*. Oxford, Heinemann Nursing.

Goodwin, S. (1992) 'Community nursing and the new public health', *Health Visitor*, 65, 3, 78–80.

Health Visitors' Association (1992) *Principles into Practice*. London, Health Visitors' Association.

House of Commons (1990) *National Health Service and Community Care Bill*. London, HMSO.

O'Gorman, F. and Moore, S. (1990) 'Two tales of a health city', *Health Visitor*, 63, 8, 276–8.

Potrykus, C. (1992) 'Guidance a mixed blessing', *Health Visitor*, 65, 9, 300–2.

Sachs, H. (1990) *A Brave Attempt: Teamwork between Health Visitors and Social Workers on an Inner City Estate*. London, Kings Fund Centre.

Chapter 3

Childminders and children

Judy Warner

Childminding is the oldest and most popular form of daycare for young children, although until recent years it has been mainly hidden away by 'authority' and participants themselves by largely being ignored, or at best tolerated by the former and by lack of self esteem and pride in their work by the latter.

When I first became involved with childminders way back in 1975 as a childminders' adviser for Social Services, I clearly remember calling to introduce myself to one childminder on the (very out of date) list I was given by the department. This woman lived in an affluent part of town, she welcomed me with a smile which quickly changed to a look of anxiety when she learned who I was. She ushered me into her house, glancing up and down the street to see if anyone had seen me. She then proceeded to explain that she did not tell people she was a childminder as it was something she was doing 'temporarily' until she could get a 'real job' and that her neighbours and friends would be 'horrified' at her doing 'domestic unskilled' work as she had had a college education.

One of my greatest joys during my years as a childminders' adviser was to see this woman's attitudes change as she met other childminders (many of whom were 'college educated'), attended courses and became a member of the steering committee of one of the first childminder associations in the country. This culminated in her enthusiastic attendance at the inaugural meeting of the National Childminding Association (NCMA), after which she suggested that we should publicise childminding more and perhaps obtain a stall at the town's annual carnival. One of my most fulfilling moments as an adviser was seeing her behind that stall in her Childminder Association tee-shirt talking to the townspeople with pride about the work she was doing.

Childminding was first recognised officially in the late 1940s following several tragic fires in which children died while the minder was out shopping. These led to a newspaper campaign which resulted partly in the drafting of the 1948 Nurseries' and Childminders' Regulations Act. For the first time minimum standards were required for people caring for other people's children in their own homes for 'reward'. The Act was overwhelmingly concerned with children's health and the safety of the premises in which the children were being cared for, and inspection of childminders was delegated to local health authories.

Twenty years later the Act was amended again, following reports of children injured and left alone. This led to a committee, and a report, and the childminding section of the Health Services and Public Health Act 1968.

The law concerning childminding was mainly negative and its interpretation by individual local authorities was variable throughout the country. But because it gave very few clear guidelines about quality of care and grounds for refusal or cancellation, most local authorities were nervous of using their powers. Despite concerns, childminders' advisers often found it difficult to obtain support from their legal departments if they wished to use the Act for refusal or cancellation.

In 1971 responsibility for childminders and all other forms of daycare registered under the Act moved from the Health Departments to the newly formed Social Services Departments. But although the more enlightened local authorities employed specialist advisers, the law remained the same so advisers still relied on 'counselling out' rather than using the law to exclude unsuitable people from registration.

It was more than twenty years after the 1968 Act that childminding legislation was actually amended. This time it was encompassed in the Children Act 1989, which for the first time brought together a number of separate pieces of childcare legislation, some already in existence, some changed and some entirely new and welded them together into one consolidated and more accessible whole.

Part 10 of the Act modified and updated the Nurseries' and Childminders' Regulation Act, which was repealed. Overall, the new Children Act has been welcomed as a great step forward in childcare law with its potential vastly to improve children's lives. Part 10 is largely welcomed by childminders and their Association, as well as Social Services advisers and their managers, as a much more positive piece of legislation.

While all this was happening legally, what was happening to childminders and most importantly the children they care for? How did childminding change from a mainly 'hidden away' form of occupation where, predominantly women, cared for other people's children, often in inadequate, understimulating environments, to what many parents now recognise as a convenient, flexible, economically viable form of daycare which provides individual care, a home-based environment and the opportunity to develop social contacts for their children?

Much of the early work of bringing recognition of the role of the childminder in the everyday life of many children and their parents was the result of Brian and Sonia Jackson's research into childminding in the 1970s. This was the forerunner of the successful BBC television series *Other People's Children*, which was especially for childminders .

This in turn led to the formation of the National Childminding Association in 1977 which, since its inception, has worked towards greater recognition of the work childminders do and the contribution they make to society. The high-quality care which is now provided by many childminders throughout the country is a reflection of the increasing status and respect childminders are now receiving from central government, local authorities, parents and the public at large. This is due, I believe, mainly to the dedication and hard work of the members, officers and staff of NCMA.

Childminding has been the subject of much research since the Jacksons' study (1979). As far back as 1977, Berry Mayall and Pat Petrie were advocating training for childminders, support from local authorities ranging from free toy and equipment loan schemes to regular support visits from an adviser (1977). More recently the Thomas Coram Research Unit project, which followed children from a few months of age until their sixth birthday, concluded that 'children looked after in day care settings even from early infancy show no signs of disadvantage in their social, emotional or intellectual development by the age of 6 years' (Moss and Melhuish 1991).

This and other research has provided much-needed reassurance to the many parents who need to use childminders and other forms of daycare in order to work, study or receive respite from full-time parenthood for themselves.

The increased necessity for more women to work outside the home, caused not only by the 'demographic time bomb' but by the increasing economic pressures on two-parent families and the increase in single-parent families, has led to a sharp increase in registered childminders from 44,145 childminders providing 98,495 places in 1982, to 106,004 childminders providing 233,258 places in 1991 (Department of Health 1991).

In all, the number of places more than doubled between 1984 and 1991. Some 1,813 children are currently placed and paid for by local authorities who use childminders on their sponsorship schemes to care for children referred by them. These children and families are already known to Social Services for various reasons.

With a scarcity of local authority day nursery and family centre places, Social Services departments have been increasingly looking towards childminders to offer not only care for children but support to parents as well. In addition to this, two-thirds of the labour force growth between 1983 and 1987 consisted of married women, and women are expected to account for over 80 per cent of the anticipated growth between 1987 and 1995. Childminding can therefore be expected to increase dramatically to cater for the growing demand for daycare for the children of many of these women.

In order to be effective childminding needs to be a stable, continuing service for children and parents. All children need continuity of care in order to develop good cognitive skills and verbal ability. Research by the Thomas Coram Research Unit (Martin *et al*. 1992) found that children who experienced a number of changes in their daycare arrangements had a slower rate of cognitive development over the first three years. These children did not fall behind from three to six years but neither did they catch up with the children with fewer changes. It is important therefore that childminders see their role as providing long-term care for the children placed with them and that parents place their children sensitively, ensuring that they are happy with the arrangements before placement, in order to minimise the chance of being dissatisfied and having to move the child.

This highlights three important areas of concern to both childminders and parents:

(a) training for childminders;
(b) terms and conditions of work; and
(c) support networks for both childminders and parents.

Training

This gives confidence to both parties. It suggests to parents a professional approach to the job. To childminders it gives the opportunity to learn more about children and their developmental needs, the important skills involved in working with parents in the unique setting of caring for their children in the minder's own home, plus the opportunity to exchange ideas with others and to find out about new developments.

For many years the NCMA has encouraged Social Services departments and childminding groups to set up courses. The Association produced a pack of training materials in conjunction with the Open University in 1986, which has been widely used as a basis for planning training courses.

Throughout the country an emerging pattern of childminder training is now in evidence, beginning with short pre-registration briefings where childminders are given the opportunity to find out what childminding and the registration process is all about. Preparation courses take place during the registration process or soon after and act as an induction to the job. Follow-on courses take place during the first year, and in-service training is available for experienced childminders, on a variety of topics, including preparation for working with children with special needs or children placed by Social Services or other agencies, where the childminder requires additional skills.

The terms and conditions of work for childminders

This has long been a source of anxiety and sometimes conflict between the parents who 'buy into' the service and the child-minders who provide it. Childminding has been seen mainly as 'women's work' and often equated with parenting, so it has traditionally been poorly paid. Childminders have sometimes felt exploited when parents are late paying or refuse to pay for holidays, or when their child does not attend because of sickness, or when Social Services are late sending the money for a sponsored child. Childminders feel this would not happen if they were working in another field of childcare.

Equally parents can feel they are trapped into signing a contract which has not been explained to them fully, or they are not entirely happy with part of it, but feel they must agree if they wish to use this particular childminder with whom in every other way they are very happy. Training in this important area of the work is therefore vital in order that the childminder can run the 'business side' of childminding effectively, and advice and support from an independent source should also be available to the parents. The NCMA has for many years provided useful information leaflets on tax and National Insurance, cashbooks and attendance registers, a special insurance scheme for childminders, and suggested guidelines on pay and conditions annually. They also have an advice line at their headquarters where childminders, local authority advisers, and parents can receive help, advice and support on these and many other aspects of childminding. This helps all those involved to have access to expert advice on this sensitive area of work.

Support for childminders

This comes from two main sources. Their local Social Services adviser, and their local and National Childminding Association. Social Services advisers have varying case loads, as was discovered in the research carried out by Ferri and Birchall (1984). They looked at four areas of the country, a Social Services division in a county authority, a large industrial city, a new town and an inner London Borough, where the ratio of advisory staff to minders ranged from 1:25 to 1:225. Since the introduction of the Children Act 1989 in October 1991, advisers have had to incorporate in their workload all daycare facilities for children up to 8 years of age, in addition to facilities for 0–5-year-olds. Although some local authorities have employed additional staff, others have not and the ratios of advisory staff to childminders continues to be a source of concern to many people in both the statutory and voluntary organisations. In practice this means that the accessibility of advisers to their local childminders is often less than adequate. The main support for childminders therefore comes from their local childminding groups and their National Association.

There are currently 1,194 local childminding groups affiliated to NCMA. in England and Wales, and over 53,000 members of NCMA. There are regional committees in each of ten regions in England, one in North Wales, and one in South Wales. There are twenty county associations who employ workers funded by local authorities. The NCMA receives a grant from central government to support their work but most of their income comes from membership subscriptions, publications and insurance sales, and from their consultancy 'Childminding In Business', which was set up in 1989 to organise employer-sponsored childminding in a systematic way and to raise money for the work they do as an educational charity.

The Scottish branches became independent from the NCMA in 1990, and the Scottish Childminding Association (SCMA) currently has 3,500 members. There are seven Regional Associations, four of which fund Regional Development Officers and there are two more posts 'in the pipeline'. The SCMA receives grants from the Scottish Office and this accounts for about half their income, the other half coming from membership subscriptions. A tremendous growth in membership has occurred in the last few years. In 1985 there were under 200 members of NCMA in Scotland, so the dramatic increase in membership and the provision of a service which is relevant to the needs of childminding in Scotland bear witness to the tremendous achievement of SCMA. NCMA and SCMA are therefore providing a much-needed source of advice, support and publicity for childminding throughout Great Britain.

So why do parents choose childminders rather than other forms of daycare for their children? Surveys show that the main form of care for children under 3 years of age is that given by relatives, followed by childminders, with nurseries and nannies a long way behind (Martin *et al.* 1992).

The needs of children and parents vary but the choice of daycare arrangement is heavily influenced by what is available in a particular area, the cost of the service and the type of care parents would prefer. Access to information and the means to take advantage of that information are very important. Parents whose home language is not English may have difficulty finding out what is available in their area; parents who do not have a car or a telephone might be limited in choice because they are not able to visit the available places.

It is difficult to assess whether parents choose childminders because there are more childminder places available or because they feel it is the most appropriate form of daycare for their child. But in a small research study carried out in December 1990 by Warwickshire County Council Social Services Department, parents who were already using daycare were asked 'what would be your most preferred choice of daycare provision for your child?' Some 48 per cent chose a childminder, followed by 22 per cent a day nursery, 18 per cent a workplace nursery and 9 per cent a nursery school.

Parents who prefer childminders feel it is the one-to-one relationship; the main attraction is the more individual 'home-like' care that the relationship is believed to offer. Parents with special religious or dietary practices appreciate the ability of the childminders to accommodate these requirements more easily. Moreover, they might even find a childminder who follows these practices herself.

Flexibility of hours is another advantage to some parents, particularly if they work unsocial hours or shifts where hours cannot easily be accommodated in a nursery. Links with the child's own local community are also a benefit that some parents see as important. The ability for the childminder to take the child to his/her local toddler group, playgroup, dancing class, clinic, speech therapy session and, possibly, continue to care for the child before and after school, and to take them to and from that school, is seen as a big advantage by many parents.

The more intimate relationship between parent and childminder can have advantages and disadvantages for both parties, but many lasting friendships have been formed through what started out as a childminding arrangement.

So what of the future? Childminding has come a long way since my encounter with the woman who was so ashamed to admit her occupation. However, childminders cannot be complacent and there is still more to be done. I believe that childminding will continue to be a much-valued service to parents and children. The much more positive legislation now encompassed in The Children Act 1989 means that childminding, at last, is being officially recognised as a valued form of childcare.

Childminders themselves need to be increasingly professional in their commitment to their work. This includes:

1   being willing to take advantage of training opportunities, in particular by obtaining National Vocational Qualifications which are now becoming available and which include standards relating to home-based care;
2   becoming fully involved in the consultation process of the three-yearly review under The Children Act which all local authorities must carry out; and

3   pressing both locally and nationally for greater recognition of their abilities.

These three actions would do much to enhance their professional status and ensure that childminders are seen as equals to other childcare workers. If childminding is the oldest and most popular form of daycare for young children then it is high time that it was given the status and rewards that it deserves.

REFERENCES

Department of Health Statistical Service (1991) *Daycare Provision*. London, HMSO.

Ferri, E. and Birchall, B. (1984) *A Study of Support and Training for Childminders*. London, National Children's Bureau.

Jackson, B. and Jackson, S. (1979) *Childminder: A Study in Action Research*. London, Routledge & Kegan Paul.

Martin, S,. Moss, P. and Melhuish, E. (1992) *Children and Daycare: Lessons from Research*. London, Paul Chapman.

Mayall, B. and Petrie, P. (1977) *Minder, Mother and Child*. London, London University Institute of Education.

Moss, P. and Melhuish, E. (eds) (1991) *Current Issues in Day Care for Young Children*. London, HMSO.

Chapter 4

Teachers and young children in educational establishments

Cathy Nutbrown

Children under 5 in Britain first experience the education system in one of three ways: attending a nursery school, in nursery class or being admitted early to a reception class. These different settings form part of the diverse range of provision for children under 5, which includes Social Services nurseries, playgroups and private sector provision (see Chapters 7, 8 and 10). Effective teachers of children under 5 set teaching and learning in a context that embodies the whole child. They must consider children's emotions, health, relationships and intellect. Teaching children under 5 is a multi-faceted role, requiring a range and depth of skills. This chapter focuses on the work of such teachers and the children with whom they work. It will consider: the needs of children; meeting educational and cognitive needs; and the issue of multi-professionalism and the teacher.

THE NEEDS OF CHILDREN UNDER 5

The period from birth to age 5 is one of rapid growth and development. At this stage children's development needs are complex and interrelated.

(DES 1990: para 54)

Teachers need to be mindful of basic human needs that are essential to children's survival and development. Young children need to be loved, cared for and protected from situations and experiences which threaten their lives and their childhoods. They need someone special in their lives who will care for their health, feed them, clothe them, create in them a sense of security and well-being, and strive to ensure that their living and learning environments are matched to their needs. Young children's emotional security depends upon them feeling a sense of belonging and of being valued. They need to know that they matter, that they have a voice which others will hear and that someone will be their advocate. Adults can play a key role in promoting children's feelings of positive self-esteem and confidence. Teachers share this inescapable responsibility and need to show flexibility and compassion in their encounters with young children.

At difficult times, such as bereavement or going into hospital, young children need stability, but all children need a sense of stability in their daily lives. Early experiences of the education system need to ensure that a child 'knows where she is'. Routines, information, continuity and support can help her to connect into the situation in which she finds herself and operates with a level of independence.

The new experience of belonging to a group comes for many children when they begin nursery or school. Experience teaches young children the unwritten rules of belonging to a group; the following comments, from children in three different educational settings, show how they see the 'rules'.

Ben (3: 11) Nursery class

> You get there after your dinner at nanna's house. When you get there you wave to your grandpa from the little window and watch him go off in the car. Then you think 'who shall I play with?' Then your teacher says 'would you like to paint?' so you paint a bit. Then you decide who to play with, then you go outside and play with them and ride a red bike when it is your turn – you wait a bit for that sometimes.

Mooni (4: 6) Early entry class – primary school

> When Mrs S. . . says 'register time' you sit on the red carpet and look at her. Not the browny colour one, that's for story. Then you say 'Yes I'm here' and 'a school dinner please' when she says your name.

Courtney (4:1) Nursery school

> You get there and you go outside, but your mum (or your dad if he brings you sometimes) has to go tell teacher I'm here, or she don't know and you don't get your milk or dinner.

These young children have learned about the social context, how to behave so that they 'fit' into the group system, and that to belong to a group you must conform. Ben felt he should do what the teacher suggested, Mooni sensed the importance of uttering the exact words required, Courtney stressed the importance of 'clocking in' and ordering lunch!

Young children need positive experiences and role models in their early years to help them to learn how they might conform and how they may need to challenge. Conformity and challenge are important elements of young children's social development, and teachers need to create a security where children know they can sometimes challenge others, assert themselves, and still be loved and 'belong'.

Children's developing patterns of social interaction often result in clashes between individuals or groups. They need help to learn how to manage their own behaviour, how to deal with being hit or taunted, how to join in the game of a group of children, how to satisfy their needs, express their feelings, and assert themselves in a safe way. Planned experiences, such as those developed at Pen Green Family Centre (1990), can help children to learn about protecting themselves. Children need help to challenge other children who hurt them physically and emotionally. For some young children, it is not always helpful for teachers to simply intervene and resolve disputes. Children need to begin developing personal and social skills that will enable them to deal with and resolve some situations themselves.

With support, young children can begin to assert themselves. They can learn to say 'No' in an assertive voice and they can shout 'Don't do that to me'. They often need to be given the words to say. It is not enough for teachers to tell a child: 'tell her not to do that' – children who are learning about language need help with the words they might say; in some cases the teacher needs to say the words which they can repeat. To be really effective this kind of approach needs total commitment. It needs a whole staff policy and adults who are willing to take time to support children through their difficulties and who are consistent in their approach. Working in this way is more difficult and demanding than resolving a dispute between young children by simply using one's power as a teacher to stop it. It takes considerable time to help children decide what they want to say and to provide encouragement as they speak to the child who has hurt or offended them. In time, such an approach can empower children to assert and protect themselves. This way of working is not about judgements, rights, or wrongs as seen through the eyes of the adult. It is about self-assertion, children protecting themselves, their feelings and their bodies. It is about children developing skills for living. Staff need time to develop the skills they need to support children and to explain their work to parents in order to gain their understanding and support too. Working through difficulties with children needs to be seen as a positive use of time and not a 'soft option'.

Children beginning school need emotional security, they also bring curiosity about the world and a motivation to learn. As they develop socially and emotionally they are also physically active learners, questioning, curious and individualistic (Cleave and Brown 1989: 7–8). Having considered some aspects of children's social and emotional needs the next section will focus on the ways in which teachers cater for the educational and cognitive needs of young children.

MEETING EDUCATIONAL AND COGNITIVE NEEDS

the curriculum should not be loaded with inert ideas and crude blocks of fact which are devoid of significance till related to some interest in the minds of the pupils. It must be vivid, realistic, a stream in motion, not a stagnant pool.
(Board of Education 1931: xxii)

Such vividness and realism can be presently seen in good teaching of children under five. The curriculum must be broad, balanced and relevant to children's needs, and importantly, it must be differentiated according to the needs and capabilities of each child. This principle is now established in law for children aged 5–16 (DES 1989) and should apply equally to children under 5.

Some learning experiences are planned, and others sometimes arise out of a spontaneous event. Whatever their origin, to be of real worth learning experiences must be *in tune* and *matched* to children's learning agendas. Without this match, what exists is teaching, not learning. The following examples illustrate planned teaching and subsequent learning as well as spontaneous events which create opportunities for skilled teaching and worthwhile learning.

Kite making in a reception class

The curriculum in the class was based around the theme of 'structures', chosen because it offered a breadth of opportunity to consider aspects of different curriculum areas. Several opportunities were planned for children to see different structures being made as well as to make their own designs. In this example the concept of structures was developed through different experiences of kite making.

A professional kite maker visited the school and showed small groups of children how he designed, made and flew his elaborate kites. The children saw the internal structures and the outer coverings in bright and attractive fabrics and paper and watched as he attempted a trial flight of one of his kites. The following day the teacher worked again with small groups of children, showing them how to make simpler, smaller and less ornate kites. She used an instruction book (something the professional did not bring), and explained that she needed to read the instructions to help her to make a kite that would fly. Her purposes included reinforcement of the earlier experience and provision of a positive model to the girls in the nursery. She had noticed that the boys were particularly interested in the kite maker and wanted to promote this designing and making experience and signal that it was appropriate for girls as well.

Following this second demonstration, children were provided with a range of materials to make their own kites. This attracted many children, girls and boys, throughout two consecutive days. Their dialogue included terminology used by the professional and the teacher. They talked with each other and with the teacher about strengthening, supports and struts. They tested for 'aerodynamics', added to their designs following 'flight tests', and retested after alterations. They checked their designs in books and drew their own 'plans' for their kites. The teacher helped with fastening and alterations as requested, joined in their discussions, observed their work, made suggestions and asked questions.

With young children the teaching and learning process is complex. This example shows how planning can ensure continuity and progression of experience. Different levels of planning were needed to maximise an experience and promote learning. Detailed plans were made to introduce the idea of kites through a rich and meaningful initial stimulus; to give clear information to children; to follow up and reinforce the children's work enabling them to interpret in their own work, the things they saw. At each level the teacher operated in a different way: first, facilitating the initial experience, then introducing further, related ideas and finally working alongside children as they worked at their own individual level. As well as planning what children might experience, teachers need to plan their role in promoting and reinforcing learning and how to use other members of staff and parental help. In this case the qualified child care assistant and a parent continued with other activities and routines with other children while the teacher worked for some of the time specifically with children interested in the kites. The theme was broad enough to encompass a range of ideas and experiences including creative and aesthetic, design, science, mathematics, language and literacy. Such planning made it possible for children to work at their own developmental and cognitive level within an experience offered to a group of children.

Vygotsky's theory of the 'zone of proximal development' is also apparent in this example where areas of learning became possible through interaction. Vygotsky saw learning as a profoundly social process needing dialogue and mediation (Vygotsky 1978: 90). These are crucial roles for the teacher.

A child exploring his schema in a nursery class

The notion that young children's learning is linked with developmental patterns which run as a continuous thread through all their thought and action has been explored by Athey (1990). Reporting on the Froebel Early Education Project, Athey described how children's action, speech and thoughts were connected by schemas, patterns of

> repeatable behaviour into which experiences are assimilated and that are gradually co-ordinated.
>
> (Athey 1990: 37)

Teachers can provide a more appropriate curriculum which matches the developmental level and interest of the child (Nutbrown 1989), by using their knowledge of schema to develop greater awareness of patterns of learning and thereby understanding more about children's predominant interests. The following example shows how one child's schema supported his learning and development.

Stuart's dynamic circular schema

Stuart was interested in rotation – he seemed to be *tuned in* to spotting or seeking out circular objects and related experiences.

- He explored a hand-operated sewing machine (with the needle removed), turning the handle with increasing speed and watching the wheel spin.
- He poured water on the water-wheel and watched it spin.
- At home his mother noticed that he played with the screw tops on containers, unscrewing and replacing them.
- Stuart's favourite books contained cars or other vehicles. He also enjoyed books with moving parts – especially those which rotated.
- Stuart sorted all the hairdressing play equipment, paying particular attention to sorting hair rollers into different size and colour groups.

Exploring his circular schema, Stuart encountered beginnings of science, language, technology and mathematics. The teacher and nursery nurse in the nursery and his mother at home were aware of his schema and provided accordingly (Nutbrown 1990).

Observation skills are important, as is the teacher's ability to match learning opportunities to a child's prevailing interest, in this case his circular schema. The teacher's practice was underpinned with theory and she understood what she saw. If teachers are to make sense of the interests of children and help to turn these into learning they need to develop the practice of teaching which is grounded in theory.

Communication with parents and continuity of experience between home and school is all-important. In Stuart's case his learning experience continued at home and was reinforced because his mother, after many conversations with his teacher, understood his actions and appreciated his learning. The teacher valued Stuart's mother's role in his learning.

The teacher spent time talking with parents about their children's schematic development, and saw it as part of her work to maintain an ongoing, cooperative and informed dialogue between herself and children's parents. Athey (1990) considered that partnership is important to children's cognitive development. She reported that parents, professionals and a sharing of pedagogical concerns and processes was important for enhanced cognitive development (Athey 1990: 66).

Stuart's schema opened up different areas of learning which the adults at home and school were able to support and extend. He encountered mathematical experiences of sorting and selecting. He puzzled over the science of movement, how things are made to rotate and asked questions such as 'why does it do that?'. The teacher planned an extension to Stuart's interest to provide further relevant experiences through a visit to see a working water-wheel. This moved his experiences of rotation to a different level, out of the nursery environment, in an event he shared with his mother and other children. He began to learn about forces, water power, and cause-and-effect relationships, finding out what made the large wheel turn.

In the above examples, teachers were supporting young children's learning in a dynamic and engaging way and fostering learning which underpinned the National Curriculum. Children were active in the process; they were working to their specific and finely tuned learning agendas with the help of skilled teachers who were aware of the children's current learning needs and had structured their provision accordingly. For effective learning to take place teachers need to:

- *organise* the learning environment to give children time, space, equipment, materials and activities which promote learning;
- *plan* the curriculum and their role in it thoroughly and appropriately, according to the needs of the children;
- *observe* regularly and frequently to build up a clear picture of individual children, the value of activities and group dynamics;
- *interact* with children, extending learning opportunities, challenging children to think, to question, discover, evaluate;
- *monitor* all aspects of their role: children, activities, curriculum planning, classroom organisation, parental partnership, current and developing needs;
- *assess* children's learning, their developmental needs, their need for support, their achievements, their understanding;
- *record* observations and assessments of children's learning, progress, needs, development, interests;
- *act* upon knowledge gained in the above processes;
- *reflect* on all aspects of their work.

The best teaching and learning takes place when teachers are in tune with children. It is based on continuous planning, action, interaction, observation, evaluation and assessment. Observing, assessing and recording the learning and development of young children are daily and integral elements of the teaching and learning process. Such activities need to be continuous and formative and not merely a backward-looking summative activity (Drummond and Nutbrown 1992; Hurst and Lally 1992).

Good teaching and learning has a breadth which includes play, exploration, challenge and diversity and it ensures that every child has equality of opportunity. Discussions about how young children learn are likely to include words such as exploration, discovery, play, opportunity and experimentation. Equally, words such as facilitator, enabler and supporter are likely to be used when talking about their teachers. Such words are legitimate and important in describing the wholeness of the education provided. However, their use is often subject to distortion and misinterpretation which can lead to misunderstanding and misrepresentation of the work of our young children and their teachers. Teachers in early childhood education need to define their terms, to be exact and precise in their descriptions and to convey a clarity of understanding and purpose which demonstrates that they have a command of their own professional terminology and are willing and able to discuss and share their professional knowledge with others.

When we talk of opportunity we must be clear that this does not mean a 'take it or leave it curriculum' but an exact and preplanned learning environment in which children and their teachers perform to their highest levels of thought, action and word. Opportunity means an assurance of equality in its fullest sense, not the 'fingers crossed' approach of providing interesting activities and hoping that children will learn, not just providing the experience, but using skill, knowledge, understanding, warmth and persuasion to enable each child to take advantage of that opportunity. Opportunity must mean that young children are empowered to learn.

MULTI-PROFESSIONALISM AND TEACHERS IN EARLY CHILDHOOD EDUCATION

This chapter illustrates that teachers of children under 5 are concerned, not only with their intellectual development, though this alone requires a set of highly complex skills and qualities.

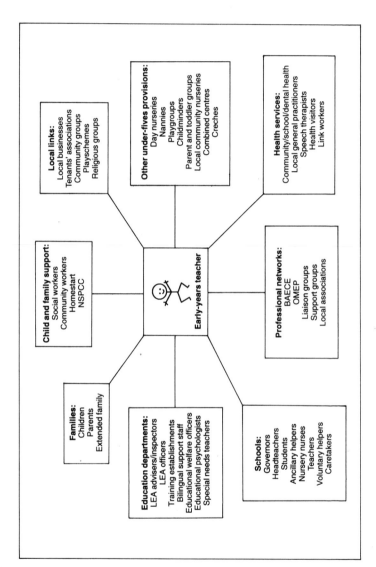

Local links:
Local businesses
Tenants' associations
Community groups
Playschemes
Religious groups

Other under-fives provisions:
Day nurseries
Nannies
Playgroups
Childminders
Parent and toddler groups
Local community nurseries
Combined centres
Creches

Health services:
Community/school/dental health
Local general practitioners
Speech therapists
Health visitors
Link workers

Child and family support:
Social workers
Community workers
Homestart
NSPCC

Early-years teacher

Professional networks:
BAECE
OMEP
Liaison groups
Support groups
Local associations

Families:
Children
Parents
Extended family

Education departments:
LEA advisers/inspectors
LEA officers
Training establishments
Bilingual support staff
Educational welfare officers
Educational psychologists
Special needs teachers

Schools:
Governors
Headteachers
Students
Ancillary helpers
Nursery nurses
Teachers
Voluntary helpers
Caretakers

Figure 4.1 Links between people and agencies and the early-years teacher

Young children come to nursery or school in their wholeness, bringing their difficulties, pleasures, worries and joys. Their teachers must often work with other professionals, and volunteers who are in some way connected with children and their families in order to understand children's difficulties, find ways of helping them and help children to learn effectively.

> Progress in education and health go hand in hand – for a sick, tired and hungry child will not learn properly.
>
> (Brierley 1980: 17)

It must be recognised that teachers of young children are not isolated and autonomous professionals, they work with a range of people who all contribute services for under-fives and their families. The Children Act 1989 reinforces the need for those working in different settings to cooperate and collaborate in the interests of the child. Figure 4.1 illustrates the range of agencies and workers who the teacher might come into contact with during her work. This kind of involvement is not an optional extra for teachers. It is a necessary and vital part of their role.

A HOPE FOR THE FUTURE

Children under 5 in Britain today will become adults in the Europe of the early twenty-first century. Our children need to think, for our world needs thinkers. Thinking children need thinking teachers. This time more than ever, children need to think about issues and not simply learn facts. They have a right to well-educated teachers who are fully equipped to foster children's early learning. Teachers need time for professional dialogue, to read, to react, to reflect and to discuss. They need time to carry out their own research as well as opportunities to reflect on the usefulness of the work of others in the field. Young children in educational settings need a quality of education provided by knowledgeable teachers who are supported by well-informed and committed headteachers.

The rapidity of growth and development in children's earliest years means that their education is of crucial importance. Teachers bring to their work a knowledge of children's feelings, reactions, individuality and learning habits. They make children's early years of education a positive experience, of worth in itself as well as a foundation for the future. Early education can foster confidence, self-worth, humanity, compassion and academic achievement, in the children who will be young adults in the new century. Such qualities are vital to our adult world, and education which encourages the development of these qualities will provide a hope for the future.

REFERENCES

Athey, C. (1990) *Extending Thought in Young Children: A Parent–teacher Partnership.* London, PCP.

Board of Education (1931) *The Primary School.* London, HMSO.

Brierley, J. (1980) *Children's Well-Being.* Slough, NFER.

Cleave, S. and Brown, S. (1989) *Four Year Olds in School: Meeting their Needs.* Slough, NFER.

DES (1989) *National Curriculum from Policy to Practice.* London, HMSO.

—— (1990) *Starting with Quality.* Report of the Committee of Inquiry into the Quality of Educational Experience Offered to 3 and 4 Year Olds. London, HMSO.

Drummond, M.J. and Nutbrown, C. (1992) 'Observing and Assessing Young Children', in G. Pugh (ed.) *Contemporary Issues in the Early Years: Working Collaboratively for Young Children.* London, PCP/NCB.

House of Commons Education, Science and Arts Committee (1988) 'Educational Provision for the Under Fives'. London, HMSO.

Hurst, V. and Lally, M. (1992) 'Assessment and the Nursery Curriculum', in G.M. Blenkin and A.V. Kelly (eds) *Assessment in Early Childhood Education.* London, PCP.

Nutbrown, C. (1989) 'Patterns in Paintings, Patterns in Play: Young Children Learning', *TOPIC: Practical Applications of Research in Education* 1, 7.

—— (1990) 'Threads of Thinking – Schemas and Young Children Learning', *Contact.* March, 14–16.

Pen Green Family Centre (1990) *Learning to be Strong.* Northwich, Changing Perspectives Ltd.

Vygotsky, L.S. (1978) *Mind in Society.* Cambridge, MA, Harvard University Press.

Acknowledgements

Cathy Nutbrown writes in a personal capacity. She would like to thank Margaret Fitter and Kath Hirst for their comments on this chapter.

Chapter 5

Voluntary agencies, young children and their families: preschool playgroups

Margaret Brown

Voluntary organisations, like all organisations, pass through identifiable stages of development and it seems that, if successful, most eventually become part of the establishment. This process can be illustrated with reference to some of the voluntary agencies currently developing in Britain in response to the needs of young children and their families.

This chapter attempts briefly to outline the process in relation to a number of contemporary child and family organisations and later to relate it particularly to the preschool playgroup movement. It ends with some thoughts on the need to work together and some of the pressures and problems involved in so doing.

The classical starting point, well documented by nineteenth-century philanthropic movements, is a realisation by individuals that there is an urgent unmet need. Like-minded and energetic people then come together to offer mutual support in a campaign to ensure that the need is met.

In some cases there is then a relatively short period, in others a disgracefully long one, before society generally supports or accepts its responsibilities for the provision of the necessary service or reform. Legislation may then follow, epitomised in the laws relating to public health, juvenile labour and child protection.

In other cases the reformers find themselves, perforce, inventing solutions or providing services, using their own re-sources on a 'voluntary' basis. As development proceeds, such local service groups may discover one another and combine into a formal organisation in order to seek public and government support. Such groupings begin to identify their own needs, e.g. for information, advice and training for the task they have undertaken. Frequently also, in the light of experience and changing circumstances, the aims, purposes and policies of the organisation are extended or otherwise modified.

Such 'services' may then be incorporated into national or local government provision, albeit often with discretionary status, or they may become regulated and supported to a substantial, though not necessarily adequate, extent by public funds. Nursery schooling itself is an example of the former process and some of the larger children's' charities, such as the NSPCC, typify the latter. The current list of British child and family voluntary organisations seeking to fulfil identified needs is very long (e.g. Cohen 1988). New ones regularly appear, particularly perhaps in the field of specific health or disability problems.

A further stage is for voluntary agencies in related fields to work together on specific issues. One example of this is when the British Association for Early Childhood Education (BAECE) and the Preschool Playgroups Association (PPA) produced papers (BAECE/PPA 1988) expressing concern about the early admission of children to inappropriate primary classes.

Eventually national 'umbrella' organisations may be formed. In this context the Voluntary Organisations Liaison Council for Under Fives (VOLCUF) can be cited, as can international bodies such as the World Organisation for Early Childhood Education (OMEP), the European Parents Association (EPA) and the new Early Education Forum.

These umbrella bodies are well placed to clarify, enunciate and campaign on the concerns of their constituent members, providing that there is general agreement on core or specific issues. Indeed if real progress is to be made in developing a national policy on preschool provision then such solidarity appears to be essential.

A recent successful example of such campaigning is the 'Law Reform Group for Children's Day Care'. This group of more than a dozen leading childcare charities, which had campaigned for changes in childcare legislation, cooperated and coordinated responses throughout the recent evolution of the Children Act 1989 and intends to continue to press for the implementation of its recommendations and requirements.

A number of contemporary child and family volunteer organisations (e.g. Home Start, National Childbirth Trust, National Childminding Association, Family Service units, etc.) well illustrate development through the stages sketched in above. It can be further illustrated with reference to the development and work of the playgroup movement in Britain.

WHY PLAYGROUPS?

We live in a village with a trunk road running through, a bus once an hour costing over £2 return to town. A lot of people leave the village to work and there's no park or meeting place, even the mobile clinic has been withdrawn.

(Derbyshire)

In our flats there's lots of little kids. You have to take them to the park so they can let off steam. It's not safe to let them downstairs without you and anyway the grass is covered with dog dirt, glass and rubbish. They drive you mad.

(Bristol estate)

He's really lonely but they don't take them at the nursery till they're 4 and then they have to go *every* morning.

(North London suburb)

We've only lived here since I left work. I have to look in prams to see what babies of her age should be doing. People either side go to work, they do speak but I don't really *know* anyone here.

(Bedfordshire village)

These quotations illustrate just a few of the great variety of felt needs of parents for their children and themselves. As Polly Toynbee wrote in an SDP pamphlet 'Freedom to Choose': 'The welfare of young children, especially the under-fives is largely dependent on the well-being of their mothers. Mothers need support and encouragement, particularly the poor, the isolated and single mothers. A young child's whole future may depend to a large extent on the kind of care received in the vital first years. There is growing evidence to show that the poor, lonely young mothers of small children are the single most depressed group in the community, struggling by and in need of help'.

One could add that life even for those young isolated mothers who are *not* poor can become pretty depressing and uncongenial!

How playgroups begin

Given situations such as those quoted above it often happens that a community facilitator emerges or more often two or more such people, having heard or read somewhere that it is possible to set up a group where mothers and young children can meet or where 3- to 5-year-olds can play and learn together. So began and still regularly begins the story of the toddler or preschool playgroup. All one needed in the early years of the movement was a place, perhaps someone's house, some toys and the children. The parents took turns in making the coffee and looking after the children while they played.

In many parent and toddler playgroups, where of course carers remain with their babies and toddlers throughout, the above description may still be fairly applied. However, even in such informal groups which may be supported by a health visitor, a social or community worker or a PPA fieldworker, issues of management, insurance, 'health and safety' regulations and play provision arise. These matters give rise to requests for advice and 'training', however informally provided.

Preschool playgroups which provide care and education for children of approximately 3 to 5 years of age without all their parents being present have been subject to regulations under the Nurseries' and Childminders' Regulations Act 1948 from the beginning. Their registration under this Act was at first supervised by health visitors. Issues of hygiene, space, safety and physical care were gradually joined by those of the curriculum; which play activities and why, how to tell stories and which to tell, introducing musical activities, planning the session and the layout of the room for example.

Other concerns now came to the fore; administration, funding, how to run committee meetings, adopt a constitution, employ staff and liaise with everyone from the hall caretaker, the primary school and the local authority who might give the group a grant, to the registration officer who by now had become the Social Services department under-fives officer.

The parents directly responsible, mainly women, gradually realised that there was a great deal to learn and were highly motivated to seek out that knowledge. They too sought advice and training.

Further needs identified

Activists among playgroup workers soon began to identify further areas of need for under-fives provision, and stimulated the development of more specialist facilities, often in cooperation with existing interest groups. Examples of developments include hospital play schemes; playgroups in prisons; provision for children with disabilities to play with able-bodied children (often known as 'opportunity groups'); provision for forces families, in hostels for homeless families; for children of working parents; and creches at courses in sports halls and shopping malls, and so on, all over the country.

With the availability of the 'Under-5's Initiative' – pump-priming grant aid from the (then) DHSS – and the 'Opportunities for Volunteering' scheme, PPA members were able to encourage the development of many drop-in centres, as well as hospital play and opportunity groups.

To quote PPA's report (1988) on the latter project, 'Drop-in centres are a focal point in a community where families can support and encourage each other, relax and make friends while small children have room to enjoy good play provision. The centre can act as an artificial extended family, perhaps with shared meals, and further support from visiting professionals and others also on offer – thus improving the quality of the families' everyday lives'.

The voluntary initiators and facilitators of such schemes rarely succeed without overcoming considerable obstacles. They need to have enormous energy, courage, persistence and political skills. They often gain this 'politeracy' and strength of purpose through their involvement with their local playgroups and with the PPA, and other training they have undertaken. This type of contribution of the playgroup movement to personal and community development is not yet fully acknowledged nor appreciated.

The support network develops

It is not the purpose here to describe in detail what a good playgroup offers the children on a daily basis, nor to give a full history of the development of the playgroup movement as such. This information is available in a great variety of publications and articles (e.g. Grantham and Grubb 1979; PPA 1989, 1991; Statham *et al.* 1990). The intention is rather to illustrate some of the other roles playgroups and their national organisation, the PPA, play in the community.

Perhaps it is already clear that playgroup involvement presents opportunities for social contacts, reassurance and responsibility for families and provides a powerful incentive for learning on the part of both children and adults. Playgroups, it may justifiably be said, offer educational experiences for children and parents, with opportunities to learn and practise parenting skills. For many families, including some especially referred, the playgroup experience offers a form of preventive or therapeutic social work. An important characteristic of the movement which should be borne in mind is that continuous waves of parents flow through involvement with it so that its influences have by now, after thirty years, reached many millions of families. In 1990–1 alone a total of 628,000 children were attending the 14,743 full-member groups of the PPA in England. (PPA 1991a). To this should be added several thousand more groups which had only joined the Association at local branch level.

Good playgroups have been described as 'powerhouses of learning' and have undoubtedly been the springboard for the further learning and career development of thousands of women who have moved into teaching, nursing, social work, management, politics (some to ministerial level), and to a range of other voluntary organisations and public service posts.

Within the constraints imposed by often inappropriate premises and outdoor space, a playgroup attempts to offer a developmentally appropriate curriculum to the young children it is able to accommodate. This will be delivered by a high ratio of adults to children (e.g. 1:5 to a maximum of 1:8) and the majority of these adults will, in addition to their experience as parents, have undertaken and be continuing to receive training for their specific roles. In 1990–1 it was estimated that only 29 per cent of playgroup staff or helpers had not yet attended a relevant course, 64 per cent had completed a 120-hour playgroup foundation course, 24 per cent of staff held the NNEB qualification and 16 per cent had nursery/infant qualified teacher status (PPA 1991a).

The workers in the playgroup movement are almost entirely parents, and the great majority have initially become involved in that capacity. From the informality of the early days of the movement, described above, the direction has been towards greater professionalisation. Most playgroups for example now pay their playleaders, on average about £7 per session of $2\frac{1}{2}$–3 hours. The paid leaders usually work with the volunteer support of parents on a rota basis to achieve or exceed the legally required ratio of adults to children.

Training needs identified

As parents set up and ran their groups in the early days, awareness quickly developed of the value of sharing experiences, of the need to learn about children in groups, and of ways their developmental needs and the needs of their parents could be met.

Help was sought at first from schools, colleges and 'experts' in these subjects. So one had primary headteachers, for example, trying to teach playgroup people how to run their groups. One FE head of department, when asked if her college would run a playgroup course, offered the services of her hairdressing lecturer who had a timetable space on a Friday afternoon!

It soon became obvious that people, often previously qualified as teachers, nursery nurses, social workers or psychologists and who also had first-hand experiences of playgroup work, were the most helpful and appropriate people to share their knowledge with colleagues. So playgroup courses which built on the informal learning taking place in the groups began to be set up and playgroup tutors to emerge.

Structural developments

Such courses have been one important catalyst in bringing groups together for mutual support and to form branches of the PPA. There are now well over 450 such branches in the English PPA alone; Scotland, Wales, Northern Ireland, Ireland and British Forces in Germany accounting for numerous others in their separate sister organisations.

The branch was an important concept in the development of support for groups since at that level it could, through its committee members and its part-time and semi-voluntary field-workers, represent and be in direct touch with its member groups and with people in the community who needed or wished to set up new playgroups.

A branch provides services for the groups, typically including a 'bulk-buy' facility (where play supplies are available at lowest prices), a toy-loan and adult book-loan service, supplies of PPA and other appropriate publications, information, fun days, meetings, conferences and courses. The object of all these activities is to ensure access to as high a quality and availability of provision as possible for all the families and young children who need it.

Local 'branches' formed county or metropolitan associations which took on roles relating to negotiation and liaison with the local authority departments and with other organisations. Gradually regionalisation took place, with representatives from the various branch levels, supported by a skeleton staff of nationally employed workers, developing yet further support services most notably perhaps tutor and fieldworker training.

It is interesting to note the similar patterns of development taking place in other successful voluntary young child and family organisations such as the National Childminding Association (NCMA) and Home-Start. Both of these now have regions which offer staff, volunteer committee training, and some administrative support to their members at county and group or project levels.

The national organisations are able to negotiate with government departments and with commercial organisations to provide vital services such as insurance, publications and information, to seek grant-aid or sponsorship for particular projects or to meet specific needs and to appoint national advisory staff.

Training and qualifications

The demand for 'training' among playgroup workers began almost as soon as the first groups became established and the motivation for learning produced by the experience of managing a group of lively young children was and is still very high. Playgroup courses are characterised by very high attendance levels and are therefore usually welcomed by FE colleges. Furthermore, a number of reports indicate the large numbers of students following other courses in colleges or in adult education departments who have returned to formal learning via a playgroup course. Many such students continue their educational and personal development, eventually moving on from their work within the playgroup movement to new careers.

This is well illustrated by a typical group of sixteen women who attended a PPA fieldwork course in 1984. One from an RAF group moved away, one had another baby, a third left the district. The other thirteen took up the following occupations:

(a) one moved north and became a tutor;
(b) one is a PPA fieldworker;
(c) two became Social Service under-fives advisers;

(d) two trained as teachers;
(e) one ran a women's refuge;
(f) one works for Victim Support;
(g) one is an NNEB tutor;
(h) two run family support drop-in schemes;
(i) one works at a Family Centre; and
(j) one became the chairperson of a national voluntary organisation.

Additionally one is a county councillor and several are school governors as well as being involved in a variety of other community roles. Many of these women state that they 'never would have thought I could do such work before I became involved with playgroups and came on the course'.

For many years the PPA set its face against qualifications for playgroup workers. Outsiders, and some inside the movement, found this difficult to understand. It seemed to be related to the philosophy that each new generation of playgroup parents should have the opportunity to help to run their own playgroup, not just the committee and fund-raising aspects but learning to lead the play sessions. The argument was that if one encouraged playleaders to 'qualify' they would 'stick around' and sabotage this 'moving on' policy.

A second reason for the PPA non-qualifying ethos had, it seems, to do with a general suspicion of anyone claiming to be 'fully qualified'. People often cite satistics relating to the number/proportions of adults qualified in the field of early years child development and education. While statistics have their uses they should be carefully examined and treated with caution, as should the concept of qualification itself. Formally qualified does not necessarily mean good at the job, up to date in equal opportunities and curriculum practice, and highly motivated to continue learning!

Conversely, not to be formally qualified should not be taken to mean *unqualified* for the work. How does one, for example, balance the qualification of an 18-year-old with two years' NNEB training or a 22-year-old fresh from four years at university against the competence of a mature parent with ten or more years of working with young children and regularly attending a range of appropriate in-service training events? Note, as illustrated above, that a considerable proportion of those taking up work in voluntary or private settings are in any case also formally qualified.

We may now, if resources become available, be on the verge of a new era in training and qualifications for early years work. With the introduction of National Vocational Qualifications (NVQs) in Child Care and Education, child minders, nursery and playgroup workers and others in what are described as 'small scale settings' will be able to register as candidates and at last have the means to achieve recognition for their experience, competence, knowledge and understanding.

The system of NVQs should encourage *continuous* learning and personal development and discourage the complacent stance of some 'fully qualified' staff. It should certainly help to sort out what Hevey (1986) described as 'The Great Training Muddle' in her pamphlet of that title. The system requires rigorous assessment procedures and should, providing resources are available to promote it, go some way to improving the quality of service provision.

The implications for the future status and pay of this under-valued and underestimated workforce lead to some interesting speculations. For example, will a person with level III NVQ in Child Care and Education receive an equivalent salary to workers with the same level qualification in other industries? If so, what effect will this have on the funding of playgroups and access for less well-off families?

Working in a playgroup

So what is it like to work in a playgroup? What are the conditions and constraints, the rewards and successes, the joys and disappointments of the job? The answers will depend of course, partly on the circumstances of the group. The following brief descriptions of two widely contrasted groups will help to illustrate some of the factors involved.

Exley playgroup has its own high-quality, purpose-built premises and is set in parkland, part of which forms its lovely garden. Equipment is of the highest standard, the staff group is relatively well paid, experienced and stable. The ratio of adults to children is high at 1:5 and the group meets each day so that children may build their attendance from one or two sessions at first up to daily attendance as they approach school age. Parents are responsible for the administration of the group, help at sessions and support the staff enthusiastically. The fees are relatively high, at £2.50 per session. Most practitioners would judge the level of preschool provision offered at this playgroup equal to the best, and perhaps surpassing that offered at a good many local authority nursery schools and classes.

At *Wyton* playgroup, the staff labour under very different circumstances. The hall they use is part of a multi-use community centre and is only available for three mornings a week. There is no alternative. The room is barn-like and dingy, with a planked floor, bare walls and a high ceiling with barely adequate overhead strip heaters. Lavatories are across the entrance hall and down a short corridor so children have to be accompanied. Storage is space under the stage, a wardrobe and an outside hut which is sometimes vandalised. There is no safe outside space for the children who come from the surrounding run down council estate, where some of them are housed in flats.

As the waiting list is long no child may attend for more than two sessions The fees are kept down to £1.20 a session to avoid excluding low-income families, though some are sponsored by Social Services. Staff pay at £5.00 per session is below the national average of £7+. Equipment is well used, some rather shabby, though efforts are made to keep it clean and brightly painted. The staff begin the day by unrolling some old carpets to provide a warmer and quieter surface for the children's activities. They then unpack the shed; bring out easels, water-tray, book-case and climbing frame from under the stage; set out the tables and chairs and prepare the play materials.

New equipment and consumables are limited by the amount the parents and staff are able to fund-raise. Although a few parents help at sessions and some are persuaded to join the committee, others have too many problems and are too stressed to find the energy for helping. Indeed the staff and supporters know that many of the parents themselves need nurturing, so a drop-in facility is provided in another room.

Most practitioners would judge the level of preschool education offered here to be less adequate than a good nursery school but would admire the levels that *are* reached in such difficult circumstances with some of the neediest children. One must take account of the personal and group support offered to these families through, for example, summer outings to the countryside for picnics and strawberry picking, the weekly lunch club, 'nearly new' children's' clothes sales, the visits of the welfare rights worker and the health visitor, the informal counselling and encouragement. There is no doubt that the quality of life of the young children involved in this group is, both directly and indirectly, inestimably improved through the efforts of the staff supported by local authority and PPA fieldworkers.

In the above contrasted groups, as in all others, the children gain and give enjoyment; through the activities provided, their experience, and so their education, is enhanced. The workers, including parents, gain in knowledge and self-esteem through their voluntary or semi-voluntary contribution to the community. They do, however, often feel frustrated and resentful at what they see, when comparing their working conditions with what is regarded as standard nursery provision, as double standards.

The majority of playgroup workers have to cope with setting out their equipment every session and of packing it all away at the end. This is a physical strain, uses valuable time and *tempts* people to limit the range of activities they offer, though many, amazingly, continue regularly to provide a full range despite the difficulties.

Working within legislation

Over the years, new legislation has increased the requirements with which playgroup committees have to grapple and ensure that their staff meet. These include the Children Act 1989 as well as regulations on health and safety, public health, employment and equal opportunities. Indirectly staff are also affected by the recent Education Acts, including the 1981 Act, as many groups offer places to children with special needs (33 per cent in 1991).

Some PPA branches indeed organise schemes to offer extra helpers and regular places in their local community groups to such youngsters. Funds may come from the local authority, 'Children in Need', or other charity or the group's own fund-raising. The National Curriculum too seems to have raised anxiety levels among parents of preschoolers who as a result sometimes pressure playgroup staff to submit their children to 'preparation for school', by which they often mean inappropriate formal reading, writing and 'sums'.

Although circumstances vary between local authority areas, many now admit whole-year groups to infant/first school in September, which results in playgroups and nurseries, even nursery schools, being limited to taking only 3-year-olds or 'rising threes'. Workers regret this, not only because of the effect on the children who have no older 'models' to learn from but also because of the group size and the financial and administrative difficulties it causes the group. They also regret, and sometimes resent, the fact that they spend much of their energy and skills settling children into the routine only to lose them to another environment where, again, the children will waste energy having to adapt to a new set of people and new surroundings. It would seem to make much more sense to support families in order to give their 3–5-year-old children *continuity* over their preschool period in well-resourced facilities of whatever kind.

Another disadvantage from which many playgroup children suffer, and which is seen as unfair and unsatisfactory by staff and committees, is the unavailability at playgroup of professional services, such as speech and physiotherapy. Granted that such professionals are thin on the ground and have many calls on their time and expertise, it still seems wrong that they may not offer treatment or advice to children in playgroups, though they do offer it to under-fives in LEA classes.

Playleaders complain that they are sometimes left quite un-supported by social workers or health visitors who have arranged placements of children 'in need' in their groups. This, plus the non-disclosure of vital information relating to the health or possible abuse of such children can cause problems for playgroup staff and possibly makes their work with the families less effective than it might be.

Premises pose a number of problems. There is a shortage of halls; sometimes there are no premises available in a particular area. Most venues are only available for a few sessions a week, and they are often in less than satisfactory condition or suitability for the purpose. Staff may have to clean the place after another community event and must routinely check every corner to ensure that cigarette ends, broken glass and even used hypodermic needles have not been left about. Everything must be put away and secured, as any doll or book left out is unlikely to survive the next youth club or other session that takes place. A small but growing number of groups (circa 8 per cent) have made the huge effort to provide their own buildings. These have enormous advantages but bring extra responsibilities for committees and trustees; sometimes, sadly, there is the heartbreak of dealing with the results of vandalism.

In rented halls there may be a high charge (e.g. £8–10) per

session and unexpected rent rises, which implies even more fund-raising or an agonised decision to raise fees. The average fund raised by each PPA group in 1991 was £606, and some small groups in particular must fund-raise continuously to survive at all.

Playgroups in school classrooms are being asked to pay higher rents and in some cases have been supplanted by school-run groups which, under local management of schools, governors see as a possible fund-raising opportunity. While it can be a great advantage to have the use of a modern classroom in which to run a community playgroup, examples of schools requiring the space and turning the playgroup out at short notice do happen; tenancy agreements are not usually granted.

The Children Act 1989 includes among its requirements standards of qualifications expected of playgroup staff. Most people are ready to work towards this, but find that in order to take the necessary training they might have to lose a session and with it their pitiful pay. They must find their own travel expenses and in most cases pay a hefty fee for which there is no grant-aid available. Fees for the year-long diploma course, one day a week, are often over £100, and some exceed £200. These are not easy sums to find when one earns about £10–20 per week!

Despite these disincentives there are waiting lists for many courses, including the preparatory 20–30-hour introductory playgroup courses for which, again, students have to pay adult education class fees. In areas where PPA has not been well supported by LEAs in the past there may be a great shortage of trained tutors, and that shortage leads in turn to a dearth of training places.

So we have thousands of volunteer and semi-volunteer enthusiasts, overwhelmingly female, who struggle against varying degrees and types of difficulties, often with little public acknowledgement to offer social and educational opportunities to about three-quarters of a million children annually. Their motivation comes from the intangible rewards of seeing children happy and developing, from the friendship and support of parents, from the cooperation and appreciation they may receive from professional colleagues and members of their local communities.

Playgroup people also contribute to society by welcoming thousands of students into their groups each year. Many are school pupils, some are adults on childcare, nursing, teaching, health visitor, psychology social work, police or other forms of training course.

VOLUNTARY ORGANISATIONS: FURTHER DEVELOPMENTS

The literature on organisational development is extensive but it seems generally agreed that organisations initially pass through similar stages, though routes may later diverge. It is interesting to note how this process has been illustrated in the emergence of several of the contemporary early years voluntary organisations referred to above. They have moved from the pioneering informal beginnings, when everyone tended to be involved in everything, to the more highly specialised, professionalised and even bureaucratic state which some have now reached. It may be said the latter often occurs as a result of pressure and manipulation on the part of major funders, whose officials may not appreciate the meaning, values and contribution of the earlier flexible, androgynous, networking model of management.

Individuals and groups within, for example, the National Childminding Association (NCMA), the National Childbirth Trust (NCT), Home Start and the Preschool Playgroups Association (PPA) have come together as outlined in the introductory paragraphs of this chapter, they have provided services, supported one another within their separate organisations and campaigned for their particular concerns. Most have developed a branch, county, regional, national structure.

These structures allow for the growth of rich, vigorous and productive networking systems in which experience, expertise and enthusiasms can be shared for the benefit of families with young children. There is evidence that, as dynamic organisations must, they have modified their aims and objectives over the years. The NCT, for example, has even changed its title from the original *Natural* Childbirth Trust. The PPA, from its origins as a pressure group for more nursery school provision, now states its purpose as 'to enhance the development and education of children *under school age* by encouraging parents to understand and to provide for the needs of their children through community groups'.

All the voluntary organisations mentioned here have appointed paid administrative and field staff, including trainers, to support the voluntary workers. All receive public funding, some having overt service agreements with local or national government departments to provide services, at present an increasing trend as 'purchaser-provider' systems are implemented. In this sense they could be said to have become incorporated into public provision. Many of them are subject to government scrutiny and influence and many of their members to control or regulation under legislation.

Multi-disciplinary collaboration

In their early developmental stages it appears characteristic for organisations to concentrate on their own business though seeking various kinds of assistance including that from other voluntary agencies with valuable experience to share. They vary in their egocentricity, may exhibit a kind of defensiveness, and in their single-mindedness be arrogant or even aggressive, in their relationships with other providers.

Once a more confident stage has been reached and/or when faced with a common challenge or concern, early years voluntary agencies are able to band together at national levels. Recent examples of this include 'The Law Reform Group for Children's Daycare' and the BAECE/PPA collaboration mentioned above. Many examples of joint conferences and cooperation in relation to training can be cited. However, multi-disciplinary training seems extraordinarily difficult to develop. Sources of funding and the conditions related to it inhibit progress, as does a felt need to protect professional boundaries.

A most unfortunate development is that local authority and health service personnel, previously available to contribute to courses, now need to charge fees for their services. For example, child protection and multi-cultural resource centre workers ask a fee of more than £60 per session, quite out of the question for childminding and playgroup courses to meet out of their budgets. This fee is charged despite the Children Act guidance requiring local authority departments to facilitate the provision of services by voluntary providers.

Most voluntary organisations in this field take a more or less active part as members of 'umbrella' organisations, such as those mentioned above, and informally cooperate when consulted by ministers, government officials or select committees. This kind of cooperation takes place, albeit patchily, on a more local basis too.

Voluntary agency representatives work together on county council committees or working parties; interdisciplinary groups organise conferences; informal under-eights forums of practitioners from many settings meet, as in Bedfordshire, and multi-disciplinary planning groups set up courses for early-years workers, as in Cambridgeshire.

Such liaison work, which is increasingly demanded, poses a number of problems for volunteers, many of whom are already working hard with the children and in their agency support services for colleagues, e.g. running the play materials bulk-buy service or visiting groups or tutoring courses. The problems are time, expenses and the shortage of sufficiently experienced personnel.

In order to attend a multi-disciplinary meeting dealing with implementation of the Children Act or to set up an equal opportunities course, to plan the setting up of an NVQ assessment centre or to arrange a training programme with the community/ adult education staff, a playgroup worker or childminder may lose a day's pay and have to pay out childcare and travelling expenses, which the local authority grant to her organisation may not be adequate to reimburse.

To be able to contribute effectively to activities such as those mentioned above, to represent the policy and views of her organisation and to report back to and brief her colleagues requires many skills. The delegate has to be knowledgeable, experienced, have access to adequate resources and information; she must be confident and not be intimidated by the setting and by all the high-status personnel with whom she has to deal. The core of such 'politerate' people within an ever-changing local voluntary organisation is usually strictly limited and the pressures on their time and energy intense.

Furthermore, it is often the case that when people have developed the above skills and qualities they are snapped up by the local authority departments as employees, or they decide to embark upon professional training. A trend towards appointing paid workers to undertake this kind of liaison work is discernible wherever funds are available. Perhaps this is inevitable as uncertainty piles upon uncertainty in, for example, the changing circumstances, responsibilities and procedures of local authorities and the funding arrangements for adult education.

THE FUTURE

What will be the future status of voluntary agencies providing services for young children and families? Replacement, i.e. of the voluntary element, or full incorporation into the public service domain seem most unlikely in the present economic situation or in the foreseeable future. Indeed if more adequate provision of daycare is to be an aim it seems that the private and voluntary sector will be relied upon to supply it. Already by 1992, 7 per cent of PPA groups registered as playgroups (i.e. approximately 1,100 groups) offer daycare of four hours or more per day. PPA has launched a voluntary accreditation scheme, modelled on that of the USA's National Association for the Education of Young Children, to encourage daycare groups to adopt and maintain high standards of developmentally appropriate provision.

Voluntary organisations are increasingly likely to be contracted to provide services on the purchase-provider model as mentioned above. Sadly, it seems that funding is diminishing for innovative and independent developments, such as the Under Fives Initiative and the Opportunities for Volunteering pump-priming grant schemes. Even if they were not, it is less and less likely that local authority departments would be able to provide continuing funding for the many successful projects which *could* be established to the benefit of children in need.

Perhaps the best hope is that at least *some* local authorities are seriously attempting to implement the 1989 Children Act in the spirit in which it was written. Attempts to review provision and to derive coherent policies for under eights based on consultation between local authority departments and voluntary agency providers of services, including training, are being made in some areas. Partnership between voluntary and statutory agencies is a very problematical concept but with *genuine* effort and goodwill on both fronts and a strong lead from the government, considerable advances in informing the public, in policy development, in promoting and sharing good practice, in monitoring progress and above all in providing high-quality care and education for the millions of young children involved could be made in the years ahead. There is, however, no such thing as *cheap* good-quality provision!

REFERENCES

BAECE/PPA (1985) *Four Years Old But Not Yet Five*. London, BAECE/PPA.

BAECE/PPA (1988) *A Fair Deal for Four-year Olds*. London, BAECE/PPA.

Cohen, B. (1988) *Caring for Children*. London, European Commission.

Grantham, E. and Grubb, J. (1979) 'Preschool Playgroups', in J.G. Howells (ed.) *Modern Perspectives in the Psychiatry of Infancy*. New York, Brunner-Mazel.

Hevey, D. (1986) *The Continuing Under-fives Training Muddle*. London, VOLCUF.

PPA (1988) *PPA Report on the Opportunities for Volunteering Scheme*. London, PPA.

— (1989) *Guidelines – Good Practice for Sessional Playgroups*. London, PPA.

— (1991) *What Children Learn in Playgroup*. London, PPA.

— (1991a) *Facts and Figures*. London, PPA.

Statham, J., Lloyd, E., Moss, P., Melhuish, E. and Owen, C. (1990) *Playgroups in a Changing World*. London, HMSO.

Chapter 6

Daycare and nursery education as a business

The private sector: an overview

Vivienne Whittingham

Sparked off by the need for services to enable women workers to meet the shortfall of young workers envisaged in the 1990s and the increasing numbers of women entering the labour market, group care in the private sector has tried to increase its share of the provision already offered by the public and voluntary sectors.

The growth in childcare provision has been most marked in childminding and private day nurseries. The Department of Health reports that in 'overall terms, registered and local authority day nursery provision has more than doubled over the period (1981–91). The balance of the provision has changed; in 1981 registered provision represented about 44% local authority and registered places; in 1991 it represented 74%' (Department of Health 1991). This category of registered provision – subject to registration and supervision by local authorities – covers nurseries provided by voluntary or private organisations. In 1990 there were 2,293 registered private nurseries in England and Wales, amounting to 60,363 places, i.e. 3.22 per cent of the population of 0–4-year-olds (National Children's Bureau Statistics 1992). Provision in this category will vary enormously in aims and objectives, in how they are funded and managed in admission policies, curricula, standards and hours of operation.

Regional trends

As would be expected, most private nurseries are to be found in the South East, where wages for women are higher and 74 per cent of women are economically active, the highest proportion in the country.

Between 1979 and 1991 the number of women in employment

rose by nearly 20 per cent and more would seek to return to the workforce if they could get jobs and help with childcare (Department of Employment 1992). The number of workplace or employer-backed nurseries has quadrupled to 425 in three years. Some 58 per cent of national provision is in London and the South East. East Anglia, the North and Scotland have 3 per cent each, while Wales has 4 per cent. Nearly 25 per cent are public-private-sector partnerships, 66 per cent are exclusively for public-sector employees and 16 per cent are solely private (Finch and Morgan 1992). In terms of registered day nurseries in England outside the public sector, London heads the league, followed by the North West, West Midlands, Thames/Anglia, South, South West, Yorkshire and North Humberside, East and North regions (Department of Health 1991).

THE CHILDREN ACT: HOW IT HAS AFFECTED PRIVATE DAYCARE

Like nearly all childcare services which regularly look after children under 8 years for more than two hours, for reward, private nurseries and nursery schools, usually catering for the 3–5 age-group, must register with the local authority Social Services department to meet legislative requirements. Crown property, school and hospital premises are exempt from registration although they will only be exempt if the regular staff operate the daycare facility as part of their job. If a nursery is a part of an independent school, each class or school must have a qualified teacher and nursery assistant. In 1990, 45,935 under-fives were in independent schools in Britain, representing 3.15 per cent of 3- and 4-year-olds.

Since October 1991, when the Children Act came into force, existing private nurseries have had to re-register. In addition, all nurseries have to be inspected yearly and, if care does not reach certain standards, they can find themselves deregistered. Many local authorities have been hard-pressed to find the time and resources to do this. With the focus of the Children Act being on child protection, many local authorities have had resources directed to that area and have not been able to rethink policies on daycare for young children.

There have been problems with private nurseries having to conform to new ratios and hence having to take on extra staff.

Although there are national guidelines on daycare which accompanied the Children Act, each authority can decide on their own standards and systems and these can go well beyond the guidelines. For example, staff:child ratios can vary widely from area to area although they are nationally recommended to be 1:3 for the 0–2 years age group, 1:4 for 2- and 3-year-olds and 1:8 for those over 3 (Department of Health 1991a).

Costs have also been affected by charges for registration and this has led a group of private nursery owners to challenge what they perceive as some of the more onerous requirements. A member of a new organisation of providers of private daycare, the National Private Day Nurseries Association, has been quoted as saying that it needs to 'challenge local authority standards and regulations which go beyond the Children Act guidelines. Some local authorities have already backed down from tightening conditions, such as staff:child ratios and facilities, after lobbying from groups of private nursery owners.' He also wants to see the Association more involved in issues such as staff training, planning, taxation and VAT (*VOLCUF*, March 1992).

A survey of nearly 500 nurseries in Britain, completed in 1990, showed that the lack of consistency between local authorities' requirements for registration had been confusing for prospective nursery owners.

Thirty-four per cent of all those who had failed to set up daycare reported that the local authority had been the stumbling block as the Social Services departments had been unhelpful and gave inconsistent information and advice. Some found local authorities particularly unsympathetic to those who wanted to set up private daycare and others found them opposed to group daycare for the under-twos (Whittingham 1991).

There were also complaints about the delays in police checks on staff and the lack of coordination between the policy of local Planning and Social Services departments. Councils were reluctant to change the use of residential premises and commercial property was too expensive. Considerations such as parking space and the extra traffic generated by parents dropping off and collecting their children prevented providers from gaining planning permission. Objections by neighbours often proved too difficult to overcome. Finding suitable, affordable premises was a stumbling block for 49 per cent of those who failed to set up.

To be in accord with the Guidance to the Children Act, local authorities must give full information to parents and providers and are supposed to regard themselves as corporate bodies where all relevant departments contribute to policy development. However, in the present climate, it looks unlikely that either central or local government will be able to combine the commitment and resources to provide effective corporate strategies on the establishment of daycare, and it is often left to the service providers to establish a productive partnership with relevant local authority departments: Social Services, Planning, Economic Development, Environmental Health, Equality Units and Recreation.

WHO SETS UP?

Many of those who have established daycare have had the skills and a keen understanding of the need for a service. They are most likely to be women with a childcare qualification and often with young children. However, they may not be experienced in dealing with financial planning and control, and this lack of experience causes problems both in setting up and running a nursery, particularly in the first year.

Costs to the providers

Providing daycare is not cheap. There are costs of wages, as the work is labour-intensive, although childcare workers are notoriously badly paid. The voluntary sector has often relied on unpaid workers to keep costs down and they and nurseries have often used those on government training schemes for the same reason. One private nursery owner in Hereford gained press coverage in the 1992 election campaign when she claimed that she could not afford to pay a mooted minimum wage and still keep her nursery going. She said that she 'breaks even' with a £60,000 p.a. turnover, caring for forty-five children, paying £1,500 a year rent and five women staff £2.10 per hour, a rate which could rise to £4.20 per hour depending on qualifications and experience (*Daily Telegraph* 18 March 1992).

The other big outlay for a daycare group is on premises, and because of government regulations on space this is not an area where financial corners can be cut. Premises have to conform to local authority regulations and suitable accommodation will be hard to find and expensive to rent in inner-city areas.

Sally Holtermann (1992) estimates that the unit cost of a child in group daycare is £3,430 p.a. (i.e. £70 per week for forty-nine weeks of the year). This includes capital costs, ongoing costs, and full insurance. In some nurseries, budgetary projections can be destroyed by difficulties in fee collection and keeping places filled. Many private and community nurseries have to fund-raise constantly to keep fees down and ensure overheads are paid. This is not such a pressing issue in other types of provision (carers who work at home or for local authorities) and affects competition between the different sectors of provision so much so that some private nursery owners have been known to complain that free state provision 'poaches' their children at 3 years.

In a Daycare Trust survey (Whittingham 1991), most people who wanted to set up daycare wished to do so as a business and were interested in having direct control and management over the facility and also an on-going income from it. However, the high costs of setting up the provision and rent could often not be recouped as the resulting fees would be unaffordable to parents. One respondent in Essex decided not to proceed with her venture as she needed to charge £110 per child per week to break even and felt that parents could not afford this. Three other nurseries in London never got beyond the planning stage for the same reason.

Funding

The potential provider of recent times has had to be prepared to devise a realistic business plan, to find out the optimum number of children to cater for, and for how many hours, to allow for increasing mortgage and interest rates and generally to enter into the world of accountancy, as well as that of advertising, to promote the nursery and attract customers.

In their report 'Meeting the Childcare Challenge: can the market provide?' (1990) Working for Childcare estimates that it costs £150,000 to set up a nursery. Some providers have approached employers, the local Social Services departments or charities or trusts to help find resources. Some have taken out second mortgages or relied on private individuals to invest in the business. Small Business Advisory Centres have advised on ways to find the investment and create a sound business plan. The Small Firm Service and local enterprise agencies and Training and Enterprise Councils (TECs) have given advice on strategies for attracting the necessary funding. TECs (in Scotland there are Local Enterprise Companies) have helped with training needs and provided links with employers to act as local partners in childcare projects.

Government funding – available from funds such as Task Force, Urban Programme, City Challenge, City Action Teams, Urban Development Corporations and Rural Social Partnership – has been used to set up childcare projects where the need to provide such a service has been tied with urban or rural regeneration programmes, training programmes, and programmes designed to help groups – such as women with young children, including lone parents – targeted as being disadvantaged. European Social Fund money has also been used to set up daycare.

The Welsh Development Agency gave a grant to open a nursery attached to a hospital in Bangor. Catering for twenty-five to thirty children and open from 6.45 a.m. to cater for shift workers, this project was so successful that its owner was encouraged to plan another nursery. The European Social Fund backed a nursery in Wales which was part of a scheme taking training into rural Gwent.

EMPLOYERS AND PARTNERSHIPS: THE WAY FORWARD

The theme of partnership has proved to be the way forward for the private sector in the last decade and for the foreseeable future. The most publicised of these partnerships have been with employers but there are many different groups and organisations in any community that have an interest in childcare. Partnership in all cases is a process of pooling of resources to provide the best service possible and to meet a need.

Employers, be they in the private or public sectors, improve staff recruitment and retention if they can offer help with childcare. In a partnership with a childcare provider an employer can offer resources in cash or kind. Employers may not have the expertise to run a childcare service but they can provide the building, administrative support, help with advertising and marketing, and create financial stability by paying for places in advance. They may also have useful contacts with the Chamber of Commerce where other, perhaps smaller, companies may also need childcare services.

Under the Children Act, local authorities have a duty to provide for children in need. Service agreements are a new form of contract with a local authority. They are part of a trend by local authorities to 'contract out' services which they must by law provide. This could be an option for childcare services. The local authority could give a grant to an organisation or a contract which could be offered for competitive tendering. Alternatively, the local authority might pay a fee for each childcare place that it has to 'buy in'. Private providers of group care have to look for continuing financial stability and that means looking for long-term ways of subsidising the fees they have to charge parents.

What women can afford

Although it is to be expected that, in a market economy such as that existing in Britain today, the private sector would expand to meet the demand for childcare places, this has not occurred, primarily because women cannot afford to pay the full costs of childcare. Traditionally women pay childcare expenses and yet only one married woman in eight earns more than her husband and about 62 per cent of all adults assisted by Income Support are women (EOC 1992). The greater participation of women in the labour force is concentrated in part-time and service-sector work – areas of low pay. For example, 74.8 per cent of female manual workers earn less than £180 per week (Department of Employment 1991). Single parents – and nine out of ten lone-parent families are headed by women (EOC 1992) – are doubly disadvantaged by the situation and are thus unable to get out of the cycle of poverty and reliance on State Benefits. Families with more than one child under 5 are also in an impossible situation.

A woman's wages cannot pay for adequate childcare in the private sector and there is little help from other sources. Local authorities may sponsor some places. Some lone parents on employment training schemes qualify for help with childcare costs. Employers, needing to recruit and retain women employees, might subsidise a workplace nursery. Typically, the employer will institute the nursery and contribute two-thirds of the running costs but, with real costs of childcare being high, parents can still have to pay over £150 a month. Some employers may sponsor or part-sponsor a place at an existing nursery. Some use childcare cheques or childcare voucher schemes to help employees cover childcare costs.

Providing a quality service

Without a sound economic base, no matter how good the intentions of the childcare provider might be, there is the real danger that quality is sacrificed to keep costs, and hence fees, low to permit the business to survive. The registration process is concerned with basic standards, but not with the quality of care.

Perhaps the most important factor in assessing quality is the carer/staff relationships. Curtis and Hevey state that

> The Guidance ... suggests the personalities/qualities and experience that might be looked for in childcare personnel but it does not require qualifications. It does not specify the minimum amount of training and support necessary to enable workers to achieve acceptable standards of care. To have done so would have had large-scale implications.
>
> (Curtis and Hevey 1992: 202)

Childcare is still generally regarded as a home-based skill and as such not 'real work'.

> The availability of National Vocational Qualifications in Child Care and Education from 1992 provides an opportunity for expansion in training and in accreditation of experienced workers. It is still too soon to know whether resources will be found to implement this scheme or what training, assessment and accreditation will cost.
>
> (Pugh 1992: 208)

However, constrained by economic realities and, particularly for some of the providers, the desire for maximum profit, it is difficult to see how many of those employed in the private sector will be able to take advantage of the new opportunities.

The curricula in private nurseries are as diverse as there are qualifications, underlying philosophies of child development and management structures. Some nurseries have managed to bring in innovative ideas. Some have been dominated by the need to impress parents keen to see their child use nursery care as the first step on the ladder of formal schooling.

A member of the Childcare Association, mindful of the criticism of the variable quality of nurseries in the private sector, has said that the Association of private providers should be 'promoting and improving the service its members provide rather than promoting the members themselves – which would no longer mean an impartial view of what those services should be' (*VOLCUF* March 1992). However, although there was talk of developing a 'kitemark' of quality, this has not yet come about and not all private nurseries can afford to have such a commitment to quality. Without an overall system to monitor quality, and continuing arguments over what constitutes good quality, standards in the private sector remain dangerously uneven and the service itself unstable. Moss and Melhuish state that

> The diffuse nature of the private sector, its reliance on parental fees and the variability and general under-resourcing of the regulatory system; and the complexity of providing high quality environments and experiences for very young children – it would be surprising if services of consistently high quality had developed. Indeed, it would be surprising if a substantial proportion were not seriously inadequate.
>
> (Moss and Melhuish 1991: 43)

But the extent of poor-quality childcare remains unknown. However, a study undertaken by the Thomas Coram Research Institute of private nurseries in the London area admitting children under one year found that they had to economise – on accommodation and equipment, staff levels, staff pay and conditions, cover for absent staff, etc. (Moss and Melhuish 1991).

Franchises and contractors

Uniformity of a kind has been achieved in the United States with the development of private childcare chains. Kiddicare, the largest, set up its first centre in 1969 and now 19,000 staff look after 130,000 children. It has an annual income of $260 million and has a policy of mass marketing and a corporate identity. This type of uniformity may not be as attractive to British parents and providers but the nursery contracting business sprang into life in the 1980s.

One company has been employed by British Rail to set up crèches across the South East for the use of both employees and passengers. According to figures on Working for Childcare's own database of nurseries, and further research carried out by interviews with thirty nursery contractors, one-third of all employee nurseries, including those belonging to hospitals and the civil service, are run by private contractors (Williams 1992).

Many employers, convinced by the argument to provide childcare but lacking the expertise to do so directly, have brought in contractors. One contracting company cooperated to create the first Midland Bank nursery and continued to work with companies such as Thomas Cook and the Body Shop. The Co-operative Bank developed a unique financial package for setting up nurseries and has liaised with a consultancy company on setting up franchises. A nursery provider set quality standards for Midland Bank nurseries and has worked with companies such as Shell and Sothebys. Local authorities, too, have not been left out. Some, for example, North Tyneside, have set up their own consultancies, as have voluntary organisations such as the Preschool Playgroups Association and the National Childminding Association. The companies offer feasibility studies, nursery design, hiring of staff and liaison with necessary agencies.

As those employing contractors do not have an understanding of nurseries and there are no controls on quality, it is inevitable that mistakes will be made. All the time the cost of the service has to be weighed against the quality offered and the amount that can be charged to the employees.

A contractor setting up a daycare service may fail to take into account the makeup of and facilities in the community and the needs of the workforce. This may mean that low-paid staff will be unable to afford the facility, no provision is made for children with special needs and little or any regard made for equal opportunities.

There is no doubt about the demand for childcare. Holtermann states that

> The full extent of the unmet demand for daycare is in the order of 2 million places (full time or part time) on top of the present number of around 700,000. Although daycare services are currently expanding, continuation of growth rates similar to those experienced in England from 1982–90 is not sufficient to generate the additional 2 million places. The market cannot provide enough and special measures to stimulate supply are needed. Such an expansion of childcare could support about one and a quarter million extra parents taking up paid employment, resulting in an addition to family income and the national economy of about £12 billion. About 350,000 jobs in childcare and early education will be created.
>
> (Holtermann 1992)

Creative solutions to the shortage of childcare and to the absence of quality control are needed if the private sector is to meet the needs of children and parents. Without subsidised fees, private childcare remains out of reach of most parents or else the service, in one way or another, suffers. A national policy is needed to consider the needs of working parents – to include maternity leave, maternity pay, parental and family leave – and of unemployed parents and students. Crucially, ways of helping independent providers to set up a network of high-quality, stable provision should be explored. Childcare is too important to be left to the whims of market forces.

REFERENCES

Curtis, A. and Hevey, D. (1982) 'Training to work in the early years', in G. Pugh (ed.) *Contemporary Issues in the Early Years: Working Collaboratively for Children*. London, Paul Chapman Publishing, NCB.

Department of Education and Science, Independent Schools Branch: Statistics Section (June 1992), personal communication, quoted in *National Children's Bureau Statistics, Under Five and Pre-school Services 1990*.

Department of Employment (1991) *New Earnings Survey*. London, HMSO.

—— (1992) *Employment Gazette* (September). London, HMSO.

Department of Health (1991) *Children's Day Care Facilities at 31 March 1991*. London, HMSO.

—— (1991a) *The Children Act 1989 Guidance and Regulations: Vol. 2 Family Support, Day Care and Educational Provision for Young Children*. London, HMSO.

Equal Opportunities Commission (EOC) (1992) *Women's Economic Dependency and Social Security*. Manchester, EOC.

Finch, S. and Morgan, D. (1992) *A Practical Guide to Partnership in Childcare*. London, Working for Childcare.

Holtermann, S. (1992) *Investing in Young Children: Costing an Education and Day Care Service: A Summary*. London, National Children's Bureau.

Melhuish, E. and Moss, P. (eds) (1991) *Day Care for Young Children: International Perspectives*. London, Tavistock/Routledge.

Moss, P. and Melhuish, E. (1991) *Current Issues in Day Care for Young Children: Research and Policy Implications*. London HMSO.

National Children's Bureau Statistics (1992) *Under Fives and Pre-school Services 1990*, compiled from Children's Day Care Facilities at 31 March 1990: England and Department of Health Series AF 90/6 and Activities of Social Services departments year ended 31 March 1990, Welsh Office. London, NCB.

Pugh, G. (ed.) (1992) *Contemporary Issues in the Early Years: Working Collaboratively for Children*. London, Paul Chapman Publishing, NCB.

VOLCUF (1991) *Service Agreements: An Introduction for Under Fives Groups*. London, VOLCUF and Home Start Consultancy.

—— (1992) 'Which road for the private sector', *Co-ordinate*, March.

Whittingham, V. (1991) *Full Marks for Trying*. London, Daycare Trust.

Williams, P. (1992) *A Practical Guide to Contracting and Tendering for Quality Childcare*. London, Working for Childcare.

Working for Childcare (1990) *Meeting the Childcare Challenge: Can the Market Provide?* London, Working for Childcare.

Part II

Children in need

Chapter 7

Becoming a special family

Elaine Herbert

This chapter is an account of the recollections of ten mothers – and more particularly seven fathers – of the events surrounding the birth of their children with Down's syndrome and of the contacts they made both professionally and socially in the hospital and in the short period following their return to the family home.

BACKGROUND

For the past eight years I have been working as a member of a team of teachers employed by the LEA visiting families who have pre-school children with possible special educational needs. The service was set up in 1983 as a direct reponse to the Warnock Report and the 1981 Act.

The main purpose of the team is to devise early intervention programmes for each child and in so doing provide the LEA with an accurate assessment over time of the child's rate and mode of learning. Home visits generally take place weekly during normal school hours, each visit lasting about a hour. During the session, the parent sits alongside the preschool visitor, participating in the teaching. The team subscribes to a 'consumer' approach (Cunningham and Davis 1985), seeing the parent as a partner, each acknowledging their complementary roles and expertise. In all but a very few homes for 'the parent' one should read 'mother', for it is they who generally have the daily care of the preschool child.

In addition to providing ideas for activities and strategies to be used, all team members are conscious of the non-judgemental support they offer each family. As the contact between the preschool visitor and the mother becomes more relaxed and confidence in each other develops, many mothers recall the events and their feelings at the time of the birth of their child. The differing ways in which the news was given became apparent. Therefore, in 1990 I set out as part of a small research project to explore these recollections in more detail.

For the purpose of the study I decided to focus on ten families, each of whom had a child with Down's syndrome, all born in the local area in 1986–7. These children were identified as having a disability within days or even hours of their birth. The families had been known to me through my work for at least 18 months and I hoped that because of this I had gained their confidence and that the semi-structured interviews would enable them to speak freely.

SETTING UP THE PROJECT

I approached the mothers directly about participating in my project during my regular weekly visit to the home, seeking permission to come for a longer session out of working hours. I had imagined that my invitation would have been interpreted as being directed to both partners; however, in all but one home only the mother spoke to me. Interestingly, in the one family where I met both parents, the child was adopted.

Ten mothers 1990

The main focus of my project centred on the mother's recollections and perceptions of the disclosure of diagnosis, the responses of the medical staff in the hospital and the support given by family and 'professionals' during the early days and weeks after the birth. The interviews lasted between one-and-a-half and three hours and in every case a depth of emotion was shown by all the mothers when recalling the events, particularly surrounding the disclosure, which remained particularly clear in every respect. Indeed, one mother was unable to complete the interview because she became so distressed.

In all families the news was given in the hospital, the timing varying from within minutes of the birth to minutes before going home. While one must acknowledge that there is no good way of giving parents such news, 'there must be ways of not making a bad situation worse' (Hannam 1988: 48). It became clear that at that time there was no policy regarding the words to be used or the timing of the disclosure of handicap and the lack of staff training and coordination was plain. Two mothers were told in the delivery room by staff obviously ill-equipped and unprepared for the task.

While one assumes every effort would be made to give the news kindly, three were told by experienced paediatricians who used words which have an expressly negative connotation such as 'mongol' or where the unspoken implication was of giving birth to a 'second rate' child.

> Quite honestly, I don't like the look of your baby. She has all the characteristics of Down's syndrome.

The other four were told 'as well as possible' by paediatricians who appeared caring and sympathetic – but the mothers were even critical of these disclosures. One can only surmise about the way in which the natural mother of the adopted child was told for she rejected him immediately and the adoptive parents had no information of the occasion.

In all but one family, they were moved to a side ward before the news was broken. While this may be viewed as enabling the news to be given in a private place, as recommended by Byrne *et al.*, it also isolates the family and immediately sets them apart as 'different'. Many of the mothers felt that while the staff 'tried to be kind', they 'didn't know how to talk' to them and 'avoided conversation'. None of the nursing staff seemed to have been given even basic instruction on active listening and no one else in the hospital appeared to hold this brief. The mothers were anxious to return to their homes but also expressed anxiety about leaving the safety of the hospital:

> It was like a fortress, I didn't have to think about what people thought about me or Jane.

At home

On their return home, the mothers' sense of isolation continued and grew, with visiting professionals often adding to it. Health visitors 'had never had a child like this before' and some GPs gave warnings of future difficulties. The reactions of both extended family and friends varied, some felt 'embarrassed', some 'supportive' and others were 'pillars of strength'. They shared with the mothers a common lack of knowledge about Down's syndrome.

All the mothers talked of 'lost days' and of a sense of unreality.

Once again there appeared to be no one who fulfilled the role of the non-judgemental listener who could give relevant, clear information and the lack of coordination between services for families was highlighted in every conversation.

When asked about the fathers' reaction to the news, many mothers recalled the 'strength' and 'support' given by their husbands but it became apparent that there continued to be difficulties in discussing the child.

I've tried to talk to him about how I felt but he couldn't take it in.

However, one very significant difference between the mothers' and fathers' role in the early days was the latter's absence from the home during the daytime – the working hours of health professionals. Therefore all contacts were with the mother who bears the responsibility of reporting back these conversations (Carpenter and Herbert, forthcoming). Consequently, the fathers seemed to learn most things second-hand and rarely directly from the professionals.

The mothers' construction of the fathers' response to the situation and the lack of published information concerned me and in 1992, I set out to redress the balance a little by carrying out a similar project with the fathers of the same children.

Seven fathers

Very soon, I was aware of the difference in my preparation for the project. It had been easy to arrange contact with the mothers verbally because of my on-going relationship with them. However, because I did not have access to the fathers in the same way and I was conscious of the mothers' construction of the fathers' attitudes, I hesitated and debated with colleagues as to the best method of approaching the seven fathers. (There were only seven possible – one family had moved away, in one there was only one parent and in the third both parents had been present in the original interview.) I was afraid that by contacting them and asking them to speak to me, I was intruding into an area of their lives which they had chosen to keep private, asking them to discuss events which they may never have discussed with anyone.

With these thoughts in mind, I decided to send each a letter emphasising the academic aspect of the study and the lack of information about fathers' reactions. I asked them to contact me only if they wished to participate. Despite my fears, all seven agreed to see me, stating this was mainly because they knew me and I was not a 'prying individual interested in research for its own sake'!

The appointments were arranged during the evenings. I covered exactly the same events as I had done with the mothers and used the same method of information gathering. On previous meetings, conversation with fathers had been polite, friendly but brief. I had therefore not anticipated such long interviews, which again lasted between two and three hours. In five homes, I spoke to the fathers on their own; in the others, wives were present and joined in.

Their recollections of the disclosure interviews matched their wives' accounts in all aspects – the wording, positioning of the doctors, etc. Some felt that the doctor was talking mainly to their wife and felt that their own presence was secondary. Many expressed anger at the abrupt and off-hand way they were told and at the insensitive choice of words.

> I've got some bad news for you, your baby's a mongol. [It should be reiterated that this was said in 1986!]

Once this word, or more properly 'Down's syndrome', was mentioned, they all felt they heard only little:

> The voice droning on, giving us information we didn't want.

All seven fathers felt they had been told 'too much – too soon' about the secondary complications, such as heart problems. They felt they needed time to absorb the disability:

> I think he (the paediatrician) should have laid off about the heart defect for a while. It was a bit too much at first. I felt I had come to terms with the one handicap but the other problem . . . .

One father, who is still angry about the brusque way in which they were given the news wanted to

> pick her (the paediatrician) up and throw her through the window.

The fathers seemed very conscious of the positioning in the room and the body language of the medical staff conveying a feeling of 'struggling, wanting to leave the room'. The 'eyes' were mentioned by more than one:

They don't know what to do with their eyes. It's the eyes that matter – they give every thing away.

An obvious lack of coordination within the hospital service was noted by all. One father described this as

amazing, there are guidelines for double glazing salesmen but not for this.

The fathers generally assumed the role of protector, being 'competent in a crisis' (Tolston 1977) and despite 'feeling a need to cry, didn't'. However, in one family the father realises he 'reacted more than my wife'.

Generally, in this small study, the fathers appear to have 'accepted' the child sooner than the wives. Not one spoke of rejecting the baby and two were responsible for the decision to take the baby home. There seemed to be an awareness of the baby having 'the needs of a baby' first and foremost.

Lack of training of medical staff

The fathers felt they were avoided by the nurses who were 'wary of getting into conversation' with them. If the 'baby had been ill, they'd have handled it', but 'the nurses didn't have much experience of it'. They also expressed concern that their wives were left alone for too long to 'dwell on it'.

Contacts with medical personnel after leaving the hospital were no more positive. GPs gave pessimistic forecasts of the future, one warning the husband that the wife

may attempt suicide or try to harm the baby

another that

the marriage may split up.

The choice and use of words again conveyed a feeling of a 'second rate' family, but now they referred to the marriage.

When fathers were asked about home visiting professionals, they had little to say except to quote the comments and views of their wives because their daytime visiting excluded them.

The wider extended family was a source of succour to all. Many of the fathers went straight to their maternal home after the initial diagnosis and found their own parents 'pillars of strength', 'golden' in the following weeks.

Information

During the time immediately following the birth, the fathers were aware of their lack of knowledge about the new baby. For all seven it was a second or third child, therefore they considered themselves to be 'experienced' fathers but they felt they were unprepared for this new member of their family. The search for information began.

Books again gave pessimistic views of the future or were technical and the fathers had to seek them for themselves. Many felt they had a 'mission' to find out about Down's syndrome but had no guidance in their search.

During these early weeks all the fathers contacted or were contacted by other families with a child with Down's syndrome. This they hoped would have helped them 'along the learning curve'. Many of these contacts did not result in the hoped-for outcomes – the families had but 'one feature in common' (Byrne *et al.* 1988). Contacts made later were reported to be more positive.

The fathers acknowledged they would have liked to have spoken to someone outside the family in these early days and one felt that a third person would have made 'dialogue easier' between him and his wife.

Very soon after the families returned home, the fathers returned to work. This they considered to be 'trying to keep some normality' in their lives. While they told close colleagues at the time, they found it more difficult with others and felt that people often 'steer away' through 'lack of knowledge'.

Since the birth of their special child, some of the fathers became aware that their attitude to work had changed. One father summed up this feeling:

> This has made me look at what and where are my priorities – the family comes first.

ISSUES

Feeling different

The disclosure of Down's syndrome will crush the parents' dream of their expected child (Meyer 1986). This discovery is bound to be traumatic and may well be the most distressing crisis the parents will face during the child's life (Wikler 1984). Immediately they are changed from being ordinary parents into the parents of a child with a disability (Bryne *et al.* 1988) and soon realise they are 'different'.

The way in which some of the families in the study were told may well have added to the feelings of being 'different' and 'second rate'. One can be sure no one meant to infer these messages but the language used – by word, body, eyes – conveyed a feeling of having produced as one mother said, 'a lesser being'. This feeling was extended by the inferences about future problems with the marriages, with dire warnings to the fathers about suicide attempts or the possibility of harm being caused to the baby.

The feeling of 'difference' is further augmented by being isolated in a side ward. While one can understand the need for this privacy, it reinforces the sense of separateness. Subsequently this is a role the family unwillingly and unwittingly assumes.

In the study only one mother stated that anyone said anything positive about the child's looks and this person was herself the parent of a child with Down's syndrome. Most fathers did not feel their child looked different. All this can be summed up by one father's comment:

> I felt she's not different. She looked like a prune – all babies do. I keep waiting for her to change into a 'mongol' ['mongol' being the word used by the paediatrician].

Information

While parents differed in their reactions to the way the news was initially disclosed, all of them felt they had been given too much information about secondary complications too soon after the birth. When challenged about this, paediatricians state that these additional disabilities may necessitate surgical intervention in order to prolong the child's life, and this has to be done within the first weeks. Another common feeling among the paediatricians is that it is better to give all the 'bad news' at once and so limit the ordeal.

During their stay in hospital the families appeared to have had difficulty processing this extra information because of the 'numbness' and 'shock' they were experiencing. However, when they went home they were ready to move along the 'learning curve' and looked to the various visiting professionals to provide this practical support. No one appears to have done this and parents were left to search for themselves. Very quickly they became aware that both their GPs and health visitors had insufficient information and experience.

Professionals often attempt to set up contacts with other families with little or no information about any interests or hobbies they may have in common other than the Down's syndrome. When a positive outcome was achieved this became a source of support and of gaining information; however, when it was not, it confirmed the family's feeling of isolation.

Mode of service delivery

Although many were unhappy about the way in which they were told, nobody complained to the relevant sources. At the time they were given the information they felt:

> we were like babies to be exposed to this. We were frightened by the medical fraternity who stick together.

They knew nothing about Down's syndrome and were conscious of the doctor having greater knowledge, so placing him/her in a position of the 'expert' (Cunningham and Davis 1985) and the imbalance of status and power was accentuated.

Recognition of their sense of dependency on the goodwill of the doctors for the on-going treatment and advice for their child also constrained their response. There seemed little acknowledgement of the parents as 'consumers' – one father felt the doctors needed 'training in customer relationships'.

This sense of 'lack of power' was highlighted in the parents' accounts of their contacts with the paediatricians in particular, but this feeling of inferiority must be recognised by other service agencies. As long as parents are reluctant to insist upon a service that responds to their needs, the cycle need not be broken. Parents in need are in no position to make such demands and the onus must be on all service providers to take the initiative and to consider different modes of working alongside families and to abandon their traditional roles of 'experts' (Cunningham and Davis 1985).

Family dynamics

When looking at the needs of different families it is important to realise that within each family there are individual as well as collective needs.

In some families the fathers adopted the sturdy oak image,

I knew we could cope.

But in at least one, the father knew he depended upon his wife:

I know I've reacted more than my wife. I just fell apart at first – she was the strong one who's taken the main thrust and burden of it all.

These differing responses within each triad may never be recognised or addressed by others outside the family and may be overlooked because of the fathers' extra-domestic employment, the traditional role of the housewife-mother and the concentration of services towards the mother and child.

Every family is unique and the needs of every member must be identified.

Fathers

Not one of the fathers in the study talked of his conversations or contacts with visiting professionals; all comments referred to the wives' experiences. Yet they all said they would have

liked to speak to someone, particularly in the early days.

Given the opportunity, they were grateful and happy to talk to me. The interviews were quite as long as those with their wives and the emotions displayed were as strong.

There is a range of professional people who may visit the home during the day and the mother is able to select the person with whom she wishes to set up a positive relationship. For the father there is never this choice, for the services are on offer during normal working hours and as such are inaccessible to the working father. There is no network set up to allow him an opportunity to speak after work.

I recognise the initial mistakes I made in my assumptions about the families: when setting up my study, I addressed my request for an interview only to the mother and subsequently compounded this error by thinking that the fathers may not want to speak to me. They did and needed to.

IMPLICATIONS FOR PRACTICE

Training

Initial and inservice training, whether service-specific or multi-professional, would benefit from the inclusion of listening skills in curricula. Further, trainers should check that practitioners have up-to-date information, and know sensitive and appropriate terminology.

Coordination of services

The more widely disseminated information is among professionals, the better. Knowledge held in pockets is counterproductive to good practice.

Accessibility

Both information and personnel should be accessible, especially for families in need.

Networking

One of the most important resources at the disposal of professionals is knowledge of resources in their area, so that they can efficiently and effectively help parents gain access to this. Parents should not be left to search for help alone.

Consumer needs

Services should be flexible enough to meet the varying needs of individual families, not 'pre-packed'.

Needs within the family

All workers who come into contact with families in their homes need to understand that some family members still need their consideration, and make up part of that family's dynamics, even though they may not be present when the worker visits the home during the day. Each member of the family plays a part; no one should be forgotten.

REFERENCES

Byrne, E.A., Cunningham, C. and Sloper, P. (1988) *Families and their Children with Down's Syndrome*. London, Routledge.

Carpenter, B. and Herbert, E. (forthcoming) 'Fathers – the Secondary Partners: professional perceptions and a father's reflections'.

Cunningham, C. and Davis, H. (1985) *Working with Parents: Frameworks for Collaboration*. Milton Keynes, Open University Press.

DES (1978) *Report of the Committee of Enquiry into the Education of Handicapped Children and Young People* (Warnock Report). London, HMSO.

Hannam, C. (1988) *Parents and Mentally Handicapped Children* (3rd edn). Bristol and Brighton, Classical Press.

Meyer, D. (1986) *The Father Role: Applied Perspectives*. New York, John Crowley and Sons.

Tolston, A. (1977) *The Limits of Masculinity*. London, Tavistock Publications.

Wikler, L. (1984) 'Special feelings of special families', in M.L. Henniger and E.M. Neselrood (eds) *Working with Parents of Handicapped Children*. USA, University Press of America.

Chapter 8

When parents separate – having two homes

Erica De'Ath

THE CURRENT CONTEXT OF DIVORCE AND SEPARATION

Family life is changing and increasing numbers of children may go through several family transitions during their early childhood years. A child may be born into a two-parent family where the parents are married or cohabiting, the parents may then separate and there may be a period as a lone-parent family. The average length of marriages ending in divorce in 1988 and 1989 was about ten years.

The number of children whose parents divorce remains fairly steady at 150,000 each year. However, this does not include cohabiting parents who separate. The actual number of children affected by their parents' separation is, therefore, greater than 150,000 each year. In recent years these figures have reflected another change: there are now many more younger children, over half of the divorcing parents have children between the ages of 3 and 9 years.

Within five years of separation and divorce as many as half the parents will have remarried. During that time some mothers and fathers may have had several girlfriends or boyfriends who live with them before settling down or remarrying. While children adjust to new adult figures in their lives they may also become members of two households – as full-time and part-time stepchildren to their parents' new partners.

Not all children move between two households when their parents remarry. Research shows that half the non-residential parents will have lost touch with their children within two to three years (Law Commission 1986). These parents, more often fathers, will focus their energies on creating a new family which may already include stepchildren, the children of their new partners or spouses.

Stepfamilies themselves are not static and while children may be moving between two households there may be additions within the stepfamily. About 8 per cent of live births in 1989 within marriage were to women who had been married previously – a new baby in the stepfamily.

Despite the high hopes and expectations of remarriage the rate of re-divorce is one in two. Sadly, many children are likely to experience a further separation in the family of their parent and step-parent. The feelings of loss, sadness, anger, guilt and despair as well as the disruption, displacement and conflicting loyalties towards the adults involved may be felt all over again.

THE CHILDREN ACT 1989

Family life is both a private matter and a public concern. The Children Act 1989, implemented in October 1991, states a legal and public expectation that both mother and father will continue to retain a parental responsibility towards their child. It strives to promote the notion that 'parents are forever', to encourage partnership between parents even when they are separated, and to stress the importance of children being brought up within, or in contact with, their own family wherever that is in the child's best interests.

The Children Act has changed the legal arrangements when parents separate and divorce. Custody and access are terms no longer used. It is expected that both parents will be responsible for agreeing what is best for their children and that they will make good decisions and arrangements. The court will now only become involved if parents are not able to reach agreement, or if the arrangements made are not the best for the child. Where the court does become involved there is a new range of orders, called Section 8 orders:

(a) a residence order – stating where the child will live;
(b) a contact order – stating what form and with whom the child should have contact;
(c) a specific needs order – directions on a specific issue of concern; and
(d) a prohibitive steps order – to prevent certain steps being taken.

If parents have difficulties in reaching agreements they may seek the help of a conciliation or mediation service. Some of these are based in the court and others are run by voluntary agencies. A family mediation service will focus on the arrangements for the children, whereas comprehensive mediation will also consider issues to do with finance and property. (See useful contacts.)

HOW ARE CHILDREN AFFECTED BY SEPARATION AND DIVORCE?

There are no easy answers or remedies to follow. Depending on the people involved and the resources available to them, children may be the 'survivors, losers, or winners of their parents' divorce or remarriage' (Heatherington 1989).

Every child is different

Children within the same family will react differently to the same event because of their age, level of maturity, gender, personal characteristics and the particular relationship they have with each of their parents. The potential for an individual child's resilience and vulnerability being moderated by a triad of possible protective factors have been described by Rutter (1983, 1987) as: positive personality disposition; supportive family milieu; and external support systems. Rutter emphasises (1987) that it is not the presence of these factors but the use made of them that is crucial.

Divorce is not a single event

It is now generally understood that separation and divorce of parents is not a single event where helpers can intervene but an often long, drawn-out process. What preceded that break-up and the ways in which the separation, divorce and remarriage of parents are handled can have a significant impact on children. Some research studies suggest that such disruption can result in schoolwork being affected, children leaving school early with fewer qualifications and finding it harder to get a job and to establish personal relationships (Kiernan 1992).

Unresolved conflict

Differences and conflict are an inevitable part of family life but unresolved conflict between parents before and after divorce is frequently associated with a poorer outcome for children (Lund 1984; Emery 1988). Where such conflict continues between parents after separation, difficulties may arise in any subsequent stepfamily which is drawn into the continuing battle between the two homes.

Diminished capacity to parent

When parents are caught up in the emotional turmoil of separation and divorce, daily patterns of family lives are disrupted. Wallerstein and Kelly (1984) describe how parental care may diminish not through lack of concern or love but because parents tend to focus attention on their own troubles. Children are likely to experience erratic mealtimes and menus, lack of sleep and bedtime routines, and less parent–child activity (including exercise and reading together). Separating and divorced adults also tend to have higher rates of psychological and physical illness (Elliott 1991). Inevitably, parents who are ill, depressed, preoccupied and generally under stress are less effective in providing the supportive family milieu outlined by Rutter.

Dealing with conflict and stress

Children's actual behaviour is influenced not only by their age but also by how the adults around them behave. If children see their parents being angry, aggressive, shouting or hitting each other they may also display acting-out disruptive behaviour or depressive and anxious patterns. Babies may show distress at the loss of a familiar adult, toddlers may be frightened and confused and fear abandonment after the departure of one parent. Young children may regress, behave badly or 'perfectly' in the belief that this may bring the parents back together. Adolescents are often openly upset, hostile and resentful at this crisis in their family.

Changes in day-to-day living

In addition to any emotional difficulties there are often practical changes to deal with as well – moving out of the family home, changing school, losing pets, less contact with grandparents. There is also the loss of any shared routines with the non-residential parent, being taken to school or doing the washing-up together. Downward social mobility and reduced levels of income are often associated with parental separation and divorce, as one income is rarely sufficient for two homes.

What can we learn from children?

Children have tremendous loyalty to their parents and rarely want them to separate even when there has been a history of violence and conflict. What all the research clearly tells us is:

1 Many children fear abandonment, and have feelings of helplessness and dependence as their everyday world seems turned upside down (Visher and Visher 1980).
2 Young children are frightened and confused and often blame themselves for what is happening (Richards and Dyson 1982).
3 Children need to know what is going on and have opportunities to talk with their parents before, during and after the separation and most of all they want their parents to listen to their worries, concerns and needs (McCredie and Horrox 1985).
4 For many the shock of their parents' divorce was more difficult to deal with than their subsequent remarriage (Mitchell 1985).
5 Open communication by both parents in language the children can understand and maintaining contact and a relationship with both parents is important (Walczak and Burns 1984).
6 Life will never be the same.

Much of the research is focused on children's perception of divorce and of post-divorce parenting. What is needed is to explore how far these perceptions are age- or stage- or gender-related (Robinson 1991) and qualitative case studies from longitudinal studies to see what coping mechanisms children use to adjust to change in family life (Gorell-Barnes 1992).

WORKING WITH CHILDREN – TAKING A PRACTICAL LEAD

It is hardly surprising that children will be upset by so many changes in their lives and that parents find it difficult to cope as a separated couple or on their own. Childcare workers have a difficult balancing act between showing concern and offering help without being intrusive; respecting parents' arrangements without necessarily endorsing a family's lifestyle; being tolerant and non-judgemental as well as offering practical help in the best interests of the children.

The task for us all is to minimise the trauma, listen to any anxieties the children have and help parents to reduce the stress as much as possible by encouraging them to work out practical arrangements for continuing the care of their children when separated (De'Ath 1991; De'Ath & Slater 1992; Leach 1992).

Helping children to work out and understand any new family arrangements by drawing a family tree, or genogram, can demonstrate the links between people in the family and a sense of belonging and still being connected even if one parent is living elsewhere (Carter and McGoldrick 1989; Smith and Robinson 1993).

Those who work with young children who are unsettled moving between two households may be able to help through discussing with both parents appropriate activities, routines and behaviour for a child's age and ability. Where a non-residential parent collects a child for weekend visits direct from the nursery or school it may be possible to lend toys and games for the child to take with them. This not only serves a practical purpose of joint activities for parent and child but can demonstrate continuity to the child between one home, school and their other home.

HAVING TWO HOMES

Children may start experiencing two homes from the moment one parent moves out. Their primary home will be seen as where they spend most of their time and the other a place where they visit their other parent. Children do usually want and value contact with their absent parent and may well be upset at leaving them or seeing them in unfamiliar surroundings.

In the early stages it may be difficult for a non-residential parent to establish a new routine and relationship with the children but children do value familiarity, stability and security more than treats and trips. Creating space for your child in your new home shows you have not forgotten them, whether it is a shelf for books and toys, or a drawer for their clothes, a toothbrush in the bathroom or a mug with their name in the kitchen. Children need time to adjust to change but will settle into a new routine if you work to establish one – going to the local shop, reading a book together, watering the plants, going to see grandma.

If the new place is too far for frequent visits then contact can be kept up through telephone calls, letters, postcards and even photos of their parents in the new home, and when possible a photo of the child and parent together in the new home. It is important for the resident parent to understand the child's need for this contact and not to make disparaging remarks about their ex-partner in front of the children.

When a parent sets up home with a new partner and creates a stepfamily household, the relationship and routine, rules and roles need to be discussed both with the children and the new partner. The children need to know they are still welcome, to have time alone with their parent as well as with the step-parent and to have any changes in the household explained to them. This is important whether their parent is moving into someone else's home or whether the new partner is moving into their parent's home.

BECOMING A STEPFAMILY

Where there is a rapid change from two-parent family, to one-parent, then to a stepfamily, this can put a tremendous stress on everyone involved with too little time for family members to come to terms with the changes and adjust to new roles, routines and relationships (Burgoyne and Clarke 1984). Equally, when a parent has been alone with children for some time and then remarries or forms a new relationship, the gain for the parent is frequently a double loss for the child – a loss of a close parent–child relationship, and of the fantasy that the parents will reunite (Visher and Visher 1980).

It sometimes appears that younger children adjust more readily because they are more adaptable and have fewer memories of the original birth family (Burgoyne and Clark 1984). Some young remarried couples with small children and no contact with the non-residential parent talk about making a fresh start, often changing the children's surnames and moving to a new area to avoid the scrutiny of being a stepfamily rather than an 'ordinary family' (Burgoyne and Clark 1984). This will have implications later when the children realise their actual parentage and they may experience similar reactions to those of adoptive children on belatedly discovering their birth parentage.

Where children are in contact with the non-residential parent it is important that the birth parents continue to play the major parenting roles within the stepfamily, whether the child is full-time or a visiting part-time stepchild. There is little research on the difficult task of raising your partner's child as opposed to the distinctive features of adoptive parenting or fostering. The characteristics of step-parenthood have been summarised as:

(a) a relationship which dissolves with the marriage or relationship that creates it;
(b) simultaneous with the marriage or relationship;
(c) creating opposite relationships with child and partner, one is biological and the other is a stranger;
(d) the child usually knows or remembers their other birth parent;
(e) burdened with an ancient and unflattering myth;
(f) where virtually no professional guidance is available (Maddox 1980)!

The relationship between stepchild and step-parent has to be allowed to develop just as the relationship between the two adults has had time to flourish. Being a step-parent is difficult when society generally still assumes that women 'mother' and men in the family 'discipline and pay the bills'. Stepmothers have a particularly hard role – to do a mother's job, sometimes with no experience of children, without usurping the mother (Smith 1990).

Stepfathers also have to define a role for themselves. It is not always easy for stepfathers to stay out of disciplining until the stepchildren have learned to know and respect them and may be ready to accept correction and guidance. Acknow- ledgement of any financial support from a stepfather may be failing to provide child support.

STEPFAMILIES AND DEATH

This chapter has looked exclusively at families where the parents have separated and divorced. Although the majority of stepfamilies are formed after the separation of parents there are still many others where one of the parents has died. In most such cases the death of the parent is prior to the formation of the stepfamily; a bereaved parent marries and the new partner usually becomes a full-time step-parent.

There are also some cases where the stepfamily has been formed after a separation and then a parent dies. When the parent who dies has been the primary carer of the child this can be extremely distressing and complicated for all concerned. Parents do have accidents, terminal illnesses, are killed in disasters or commit suicide. The children have to cope with the suddenness or the stress of illness and then death of their parent. They may also find themselves immediately transferred to live with their other parent, with whom they may have had little or no contact, and a step-parent and step-siblings they may have never met.

The new step-parent may be confronted with a situation he or she had not imagined taking on – being the full-time step-parent. In some cases the children are living with a step-parent who wants to keep them in the house they were familiar with but if no appropriate legal arrangements have been made this may not be possible.

It is clearly important that any stepfamily with young children work out in advance with all the adults involved, and the children if they are old enough to understand, what arrangements will be made should either of the birth parents die. The Children Act does provide for such arrangements to be formalised in the best interest of the children.

IN CONCLUSION

Increasing numbers of children are experiencing the separation and divorce of their parents and will be moving between two households as they maintain contact with each parent. In order for children to benefit from such arrangements it is important that parents reduce conflict between themselves in front of the children, keep the children informed about arrangements, talk to them in language they can understand and take time to listen to their own feelings and concerns.

Young children value familiarity and stability in their lives and routines should be established so they can feel secure in whichever home they happen to be. Feeling at home means knowing what the rules are, having a space to call your own and to keep personal belongings. Children can accept that their parents live in different places and grow up feeling loved and lovable providing parents communicate their love and commitment to them in a reliable, safe and caring way. Children will show signs of stress and distress when their parents are separating and this is normal behaviour which should be understood, supported, listened to and worked through.

REFERENCES

Burgoyne, J. and Clark, D. (1984) *Making a Go of It, A Study of Stepfamilies in Sheffield*. London, Routledge & Kegan Paul.

Carter, E. and McGoldrick, M. (eds) (1989) *The Family Life Cycle: A Framework for Family Therapy*. USA, Gardner Press.

De'Ath, E. (1991) *Changing Families: A Guide for Early Years Workers. VOLCUF Starting Points 10*. London, VOLCUF or STEPFAMILY.

De'Ath, E. and Slater, D. (1992) *Parenting Threads, Caring for Children when Couples Part*. London, STEPFAMILY publications.

Elliott, V.J. (1991) *Divorce and Adult Health: The Mediating Effects of Gender*. Cambridge, Child Care and Development Group paper.

Emery, Robert (1988) *Marriage, Divorce and Children's Adjustment*. London, Sage.

Gorell-Barnes, G. (1992) 'Growing up in stepfamilies: some preliminary observations', in E. De'Ath (ed.) *Stepfamilies Today: What Do We Know? What Do We Need to Know?*. Croydon, Significant Publications.

Heatherington, E.M. (1989) 'Coping with family transitions: winners, loser and survivors', *Child Development*, 60, 1–14.

Kiernan, K. (1992) *The Impact of Family Disruption in Childhood on Transitions Made in Young Adult Life. Population studies, Vol. 46*. London, HMSO.

Law Commission (1986) *150,000 Children Each Year: Who Cares?*. London, HMSO.

Leach, P. (ed.) (1992) *Stress in Young Children's Lives*. London, VOLCUF.

Lund, M. (1984) 'Research on divorce and children', *Family Law*, 14 (Sept.), 198–201.

McCredie, G. and Horrox, A. (1985) *Voices in the Dark, Children and Divorce*. London, Unwin Paperbacks.

Maddox, B. (1980) *Step-parenting, How to Live with Other People's Children*. London, Unwin Paperbacks.

Mitchell, A. (1985) *Children in the Middle: Living Through Divorce*. London, Tavistock Publications.

Richards, M. and Dyson, M. (1982) *Separation, Divorce and the Development of Children: A Review*. London, DHSS (unpublished).

Robinson, M. (1991) *Family Transformation Through Divorce and Remarriage: A Systemic Approach*. London, Routledge.

Rutter, M. (1983) 'Stress, coping, and development: some issues and some questions', in N. Garmezy and M. Rutter (eds) *Stress, Coping and Development in Children*. New York, McGraw-Hill.

—— (1987) 'Psychosocial resilience and protective mechanisms', *American Journal of Orthopsychiatry*, 57, 316–31.

Smith, D. (1990) *Stepmothering*. London, Harvester Wheatsheaf.

Smith, D. and Robinson, M. (1993) *Step by Step: Focus on Stepfamilies*, Hemel Hempstead, Simon and Schuster.

Tugendaht, J. (1990) *What Teenagers can tell us about Divorce and Stepfamilies*. London, Bloomsbury.

Visher, E.B. and Visher, J.S. (1980) *Stepfamilies, Myths and Realities*. New Jersey, Citadel Press.

Walczak, Y. and Burns, S. (1984) *Divorce: the Child's Point of View*. London, Harper & Row.

Wallerstein, J.S. and Kelly, J.B. (1984) *Surviving the Breakup, How Children and Parents Cope with Divorce*. London, Grant McIntyre.

USEFUL CONTACTS

National Family Mediation Council
Solicitors Family Law Association
STEPFAMILY – Helpline 071–372 0846

Chapter 9

Supporting 'children in need' – the role of the social worker

Norma Baldwin and Christine Harrison

INTRODUCTION

All professionals in the field of child education, health and welfare will have been aware of the expectations which accompanied the implementation of the Children Act 1989. There was an 'unprecedented exercise to inform and disseminate widely' its requirements (Department of Health 1992). More than £2 million was spent on ten volumes of guidance to support the Act and almost £1 million on information for parents and children. This 'most comprehensive and far reaching reform of child care law . . . in living memory' (The Lord Chancellor, House of Lords, 6 December 1988) was heralded as a radical resolution of a diverse range of crises which had dogged social work within the field of childcare since the inquiry into the death of Maria Colwell in 1974 (Department of Health and Social Security 1974; Stevenson 1992). The Act was received by practitioners with a mixture of hope and appre- hension. Unrestrained optimism was always misplaced, yet rigorous critical evaluation of the opportunities and problems it brings is still in its infancy (Freeman 1992; Parton 1991; Masson 1992).

In theory, this fundamental reform of the framework of child-care law, informed by the recommendations of the Short Report and the principles of the White Paper, *The Law on Child Care and Family Services* (Department of Health and Social Security 1987), provides a new set of imperatives for social work intervention with children and families, as well as for inter-professional work:

1 support for children and their families;
2 working in partnership with parents and children;
3 using the least intrusive way of intervening; and
4 protecting from harm.

In practice, however, each of these may be the subject of varied and tendentious interpretation. Both Michael Freeman and Nigel Parton have scrutinised not just what the Act says, but what it represents in terms of shifts in the relationships between the state, the family, and children and young people. While a legal framework provides a basic structure and responsibilities, and may give important messages, there are broader issues relating to social policy, social and economic divisions, attitudes to children and families, which need to be taken into account. Social workers and other health and welfare professionals are the mediators between the state and families and children, representing in complex ways the relationships between policy, law, social attitudes and behaviour. Individual social workers are representatives of agencies with responsibilities, powers and resources to control, support and monitor the behaviour of children and families. They do not act in isolation, but as members of organisations, accountable to their employers as well as to the children and families they work with, subject to many contradictory pressures.

Arguably, these broader issues have as much, if not more, impact on the form and shape of social work practice in childcare as the legal framework, and contribute significantly to some of the difficulties and dilemmas inherent in the social worker's role.

CONTEXT

This chapter will consider, against the backdrop of this complex combination of legal, social, ideological and professional factors, the responsibilities of local authorities and *the role of the local authority social worker in supporting children and young people within their families and in protecting their needs and interests.* Drawing on critical appreciations of the Children Act, it will attempt to identify opportunities the Act may afford for progressive practice. It will ask what is the best practice we should expect and how the Act can be used to generate this. It will take the view that a basic prerequisite for promoting the needs and interests of children and young people is the establishment of *a broad overview of the needs of all children and young people in society.* This must include a consideration of the economic and social conditions which promote development, and on which parents are dependent to care effectively, as well as an understanding of the material conditions and social attitudes which impede development and undermine parents' abilities to care for their children. It may be useful, therefore, to conceptualise child protection as being about promoting the interests and well-being of all children, rather than focusing narrowly on the perceived inadequacies of parents, and to take as a starting point David Gil's definition that

> any act of commission or omission by individuals, institutions, or society as a whole, and any condition resulting from such acts or inaction, which deprive children of equal rights and liberties, and/or interfere with their optimal development, constitute, by definition, abusive acts or conditions.
>
> (Gil 1970: 17)

This allows us to consider a whole range of factors which contribute to adversity or harm in childhood – from poverty, inadequate housing and education, environmental deficits to institutional and individual racism, sexism and abuse.

ROLES, TASKS AND RESPONSIBILITIES

The Children Act sets a new agenda for the range of services to be provided by Social Services departments and for the involvement of social workers in the lives of children and their families. New roles, tasks and responsibilities are established by the legal and administrative framework of the Act together with associated regulations. The general duties of local authorities include the following:

1 to investigate the circumstances of children who are believed to be at risk of harm;
2 to promote the upbringing of children in need by their families, wherever possible without making a legal order;
3 to provide services for children with disabilities and their families;
4 to work in partnership with parents;
5 to take into account the child or young person's views as well as their cultural, religious and linguistic background;
6 to provide acceptable, non-stigmatised responses to the normal problems of family life, through a range and level of services appropriate to the needs of children, including children with disabilities, in their area;
7 to review and regulate daycare for under-eights;

8 to safeguard and promote the welfare of children in community homes, children's homes, to register private homes, and to promote the welfare of children in boarding schools; and
9 to advise, assist and befriend children in care, with a view to reintegrating them into their families or the community.

Additionally, practitioners are urged in the direction of good practice through comprehensive guidance which followed closely on the heels of the Act, 'distilled from research and practice wisdom' (Department of Health 1989: 1).

Many social workers and other workers involved in childcare or child protection work are uncertain of the relationship between the law, regulations and guidance and what this means for them, their agency, their practice. This relationship is clearly and usefully articulated in *The Care of Children: Principles and Practice in Regulations and Guidance* (Department of Health 1989) and is summarised in Table 9.1.

Alternatively, law and regulations tell us what is to be provided and codes and guidance give very strong signals about how it will be provided.

In this chapter we are concentrating on the role of social workers as individuals, rather than the role of local authorities. It is, however, important to remember the relationship between them and the context within which they work. This can best be illustrated diagrammatically, as in Figure 9.1.

Three main aspects of the role of the social worker will be given detailed consideration, in relation to:

1 children in need;
2 assessment; and
3 investigation of alleged harm.

In doing so, underlying themes and principles will be drawn out, particularly:

(a) partnership;
(b) rights; and
(c) paramountcy of the child's interests.

Table 9.1 The relationship between the law, regulations and guidance

Regulations say	*you must, you shall do.*
Codes of practice say	*you ought, you should.*
Guidance (which explains regulations) says	*you must.*
Guidance (which sets out good practice) says	*it is highly desirable to, unless there is good reason not to, you should.*

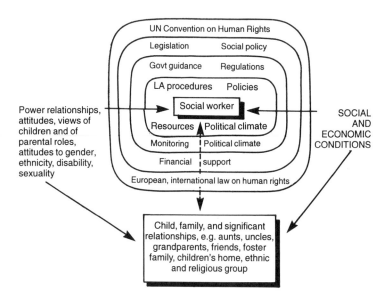

Figure 9.1 The role of the social worker – ecological factors

CHILDREN IN NEED AND THE SOCIAL WORKER

The concept of children in need has been defined and used for the first time in the Children Act. A general definition is provided by section 17(10): that a child is in need if his or her health or development would not be maintained, or would be impaired, without the services of the local authority, or he or she has a disability. Arising from this definition local authorities are expected to take steps to identify children living in their area who are in need and a range of general and specific responsibilities are placed on the local authority to promote the development of children and young people in these circumstances. Part III of the Act, together with Schedule 2, describes these responsibilities and the sort of provision that should be made. The philosophy and rationale underpinning this provision is that children are best cared for within their families, and that where help is required to do this, it should be given on an agreed basis. The first responsibility of the local authority social worker, therefore, is to provide the sort of support and services which would ensure this.

The range of services and support which could be provided is extensive, and includes:

1 assistance in cash or kind;
2 daycare and training, advice, guidance for those providing daycare;
3 accommodation for children and young people who have no one to look after them or whose carer is unable to care for them;
4 a register of children with disabilities;
5 provision for children with disabilities;
6 provision to reduce the need for care or criminal proceedings;
7 for children living with their families – advice, guidance, counselling, social and cultural activities;
8 family centres;
9 help to enable a child or young person who is living apart from her/his family to return home;
10 financial or other assistance to ensure that an alleged abuser can leave a family home; and
11 services to prevent children from suffering harm or neglect.

This aspect of the role of the social worker is potentially very positive, based as it is on a much broader definition of preventive social work than was previously contained in childcare legislation. Optimism about the effectiveness of these provisions, however, may be limited on a number of fronts.

The discretionary nature of much of the provision

The state may, but is not obliged to provide services. Families may have little opportunity for defining the sorts of input which would be most useful to them. At worst, services may be provided in ways that increase surveillance and undermine parental confidence. 'In some cases intervention by offer of services may be little different from action under a court order, because services are provided on the understanding that failure to cooperate will lead to court proceedings' (Masson 1992: 105).

The context in which the need arises

When consideration is given to other areas of social policy, for example, income maintenance, health, housing, and employment, and the impact of these on children's lives, then it becomes clear that the significance of the Children Act for an individual family will be small, however assiduous a social worker might be in trying to obtain services and resources.

Definitions of need

These may reflect resource limitations, and therefore carry the risk of being stigmatising and discriminatory. A parent desperately in need of the relief offered by a nursery place may find this difficult to accept, if priority is given to children deemed to be 'at risk'.

In these circumstances the role of the individual social worker may be severely constrained. While charged with the responsibility of promoting the best interests of the child, in practice she may have little room for manoeuvre, and be pressurised into defensive and limited adherence to those sorts of work which departmental priorities and statutory responsibilities dictate. This is particularly common in social work teams where the weight of cases where children are thought to have been harmed has displaced preventive work (Stevenson 1992).

ASSESSMENT

If the social worker has a central role in supporting children in need or in adversity, then assessment is the central process through which the needs of children and their families may be identified and necessary resources provided. Assessment relates to the general care of children (Grimshaw and Sumner 1991: vi). It is not just about assessing the risk of abuse, but about looking at what is required to promote the full development of children.

General societal expectations are that parents will meet the needs of children, irrespective of the circumstances that they find themselves in. Most parents, in fact, have these expectations of themselves (Gill 1992). Simply expressed, assessment is about formulating a view of a child's needs and what resources would be required to enable parents to provide safe care.

Clearly, individuals, both adults and children, have complex and inter-related needs – physical, emotional, social and developmental. The interactions and relationships that go to make up the day-to-day life of a child in a particular family will have been shaped by a number of factors and experiences, both current and historical (Holman 1988; Brown and Madge 1982). Because of this, while assessment may be a simple concept, it is a complex and dynamic process rather than the mechanical, value-free collection of information. It will have different levels – societal, community and individual – and different dimensions, such as individual and family histories. It will need to take account of the impact on caring for children of material factors such as poor housing and poverty, as well as ideological factors such as racism, sexism and homophobia. It will be dependent on close inter-agency understandings and collaboration.

The Guidance accompanying the Children Act emphasises that assessment is something which should be done *with* a family and not *on* a family (Department of Health 1991a). There are many compelling reasons for such good but not always appreciated advice. As Owen Gill's (1992) study in Bristol and the work of the Henley Safe Children project (NSPCC/University of Warwick 1993) in Coventry have demonstrated, parents and children are experts on their own situations. Not only are they able to identify sources of difficulty in their lives, they have ideas about how these can be sorted out. If assessment is not undertaken in a way which incorporates parents' and children's perspectives, then it is likely to be partial.

If assessment is to lead to specific plans for families, children or communities these are unlikely to be successful unless there is some sharing or agreement over the content or the aims and objectives. This is as valid where the assessment has been generated by an unexplained injury as where it follows a request for respite care for a child with disabilities or an application from people who want to become foster parents.

INVESTIGATION OF ALLEGED HARM

The pivotal role of the social worker in child protection – in the investigation of possible instances of physical, emotional or sexual abuse – is perhaps one of the most publicly debated and commented upon aspects of their work. In a number of notable inquiries during the 1980s (Beckford, Carlile, Henry), the social workers involved attracted close scrutiny and criticism. They were found to have given insufficient attention to the child in question, and to have misunderstood their legal responsibilities. At the other end of the spectrum, there have also been occasions, in the Cleveland, Orkney and Rochdale inquiries, when social workers have been accused of acting precipitately, carelessly overriding the rights of parents. It was not just social workers who were the subject of trenchant criticism; other agencies, personnel and the nature of interagency collaboration also attracted considerable opprobrium. There was also an appreciation that the collection of provisions which constituted the previous legal framework for childcare was both unnecessarily complex and inherently flawed (Eekelaar and Dingwall 1990).

For these reasons, the sections of the Children Act which describe the social worker's role in child protection were much debated during drafting stages (Parton 1991). The aim was to provide a framework which would offer protection to children and young people, but at the same time preclude unnecessary intrusion into the lives of families; to construct some new balance between the rights of parents and the rights of children. It had to ensure that social workers could deal with emergency situations, where children were at immediate risk of harm, but at the same time place some check on the excessive use of power.

Section 47 of the Children Act 1989 requires that a local authority make enquiries if there is reasonable cause to suspect that a child in their area is suffering or is likely to suffer significant harm, or is the subject of police protection or an emergency protection order. On the basis of these investigations the local authority must decide what further action needs to be taken to safeguard or promote the child's welfare. This could include providing the sorts of services already mentioned available under Part III of the Act, or consideration of whether further legal proceedings need to be initiated.

Social workers are not the only workers, and their agencies not the only agencies, that are involved when it is thought that a child has suffered harm. The significance of the role of inter-agency cooperation and collaboration is indicated by the requirement within the Act that, when a local authority is conducting an investigation a duty is placed on a range of agencies to help. This is elaborated upon in *Working Together* (Department of Health 1991b) and police, education, probation and health professionals will all be centrally involved. In each local authority area a child protection committee, made up of representatives of all agencies which might have some involvement in child protection work, is responsible for developing detailed procedures to guide workers through initial investigations and subsequent action.

At the same time as investigations are being carried out under these requirements, it is likely that parallel investigations will be undertaken to establish whether criminal charges can be brought. A particular aspect of inter-agency collaboration, then, is the involvement of the police in the interview process. The widespread policy of joint interviewing by a social worker and police officer, which developed specifically in the investigation of child sexual abuse has become well established and used for investigations of physical abuse as well. The recent Home Office document *Memorandum of Good Practice* gives guidelines about how children who are witnesses can be interviewed in ways which meet evidential requirements, including the use of video-taped evidence. Increasingly the social worker's role of undertaking investigations in a way which takes account of the needs, feelings and views of a child or young person has been overtaken by evidential considerations which may be in opposition. The judicial process, with its elaborate but clear legal requirements, is likely to have more power to dictate or prescribe the process and priorities of an investigation than the much more nebulous concept of the child's welfare, or sensitivity to the child's wishes, needs or interests.

Nigel Parton (1991) has described a discourse of 'legalism' as characterising the nature of the debate on the formulation and implementation of the Children Act. Within such a discourse, it is argued, too great an emphasis is placed on conforming to rules and on the role of the social worker as an agent of the law, at the expense of other considerations. Social work training, together with the high level of public and professional interest, has ensured that social workers are more aware than ever before of their legal responsibilities. Corinne Wattam (1992) illustrates how investigative work in child protection is a matter, not simply of unwavering adherence to government guidelines and legal requirements, but their sensitive, skilled and careful interpretation in the light of a child's particular circumstances and needs. 'There is no single right way of responding to abused children. It is important to give serious consideration to the differences between children and their experience and to use the legal processes if it is appropriate' (Christopher Brown, introduction to Wattam 1992: vi). The Children Act is unequivocal that the child's interests must be paramount.

The social worker's role in recognising how difficult it may be for children to talk about painful events with strangers, and how lengthy a process of building up trust may be, is crucial. It may be difficult to reconcile the demands of a legal process with the confused reality of a child, experiencing hurt and distress, conflicting loyalties, and fear of future consequences. At times, being child-centred may be incompatible with the evidential requirements of legal proceedings, and it is not self-evident that children's interests are always served by the prosecution of abusers. In many cases, evidence will not be sufficient to bring about a conviction. The delay in hearing a case, and the trauma of having to appear as a witness (Flin 1991), may seriously impede the child's journey to recovery. It is important to appreciate that the focus of a criminal investigation is different from that of a social work investigation. Conflating the two, and treating them as one and the same thing, may frustrate the social work task and ultimately constitute another abusive experience for the child.

The task of investigation for the social worker centres on crisis intervention and protecting the rights and interests of individual children. It can play little part in the *general* promotion of children's welfare, unless broader lessons are drawn which can have some impact on the societal conditions in which harm to children arises. This in turn reinforces the view that assessment should be focused both on individual needs, and those of children and their families and communities generally (Gill 1992; NSPCC/ University of Warwick 1993).

PROMOTING POSITIVE PRACTICE

The complexity of the role of the social worker in supporting 'children in need' has been stressed. Some of the principles and dilemmas implicit in our discussion and descriptions deserve explicit consideration and evaluation.

Discussion about openness, honesty and working in partnerships with parents, children, and young people are not recent developments in social work (Shemmings 1991; Family Rights Group 1991). These discussions have been imbued with a certain urgency and force since the implementation of the Children Act, making more frequent appearances in the everyday conversations of social workers.

The term partnership is not actually used within the Act, although it permeates the accompanying regulations and guidance. It was a principle which informed the influential White Paper *The Law on Child Care and Family Services* (Department of Health and Social Security 1987), as this illustrative quotation demonstrates:

> A distinction is often drawn between the interests of children and the interests of their parents. In the great majority of families, including those who are for one reason or another in need of social services, this distinction does not exist. The interests of the children are best served by their remaining with their families and the interests of their parents best served by allowing them to undertake their natural and legal responsibility to care for their own children. Hence the focus effort should be to enable and assist parents to discharge those responsibilities. Even when a child has to spend some time away from home, every effort should be made to maintain and foster links between the child and family and to care for the child in partnership rather than in opposition to parents and to work towards the child's return home.
>
> (Department of Health and Social Security 1987)

Many of the detailed provisions of the Children Act presuppose a high level of consultation and partnership.

However, the evidence derived from a whole range of research within the childcare field over the last ten years powerfully demonstrates that yawning gaps exist between the aims and objectives of childcare services and the reality and consequences for individuals, families and groups (Department of Health 1991c).

Perhaps the most potent and significant undermining influence is manifest where social workers themselves use the term 'partnership' euphemistically, without any concerted attempt to look at what it means, why it should be pursued and how it can be promoted as a part of empowerment-based work.

The essential debate about the nature of so many social work relationships is encapsulated as follows:

> The term partnership seems set to become the buzzword for the 90's although some have questioned the use of such a word in situations where the distribution of power is clearly unequal. For power is what we are really talking about – the redistribution of power from the very powerful (professionals) to the powerless (families and children). This will require service providers to be willing to give up some of their power.
>
> (Family Rights Group 1991)

A realistic appraisal of the concept of partnership recommends some recognition that the transfer or equalisation of power will always be limited by legal requirements and the need to promote and protect the interests of children and young people. Being clear and explicit about this, resisting the temptation to describe as 'partnership' approaches which would be more accurately described as 'degrees of tokenism' or 'non-participation' may be more likely to encourage empowerment-based work. Where parents and young people have sufficient information to be able to understand what is happening, they can contribute to planning and have some power to influence the outcome. Where the more powerful person in the partnership is aware of this, attempts can be made to counteract those aspects of oppression inherent in the relationship, and to be willing and committed to act to maximise the resources, skills and knowledge that the less powerful person has access to (Family Rights Group 1991).

The principle of treating the child's welfare as paramount depends on adequate recognition of these factors by individual social workers. But however powerful they may appear in relation to vulnerable children and families, they have only the power vested in them by their agencies. Empowerment can only come when local authorities are able to pay realistic attention to those factors which harm children's development, and those which sustain families and help them cope with the everyday problems of family life (Department of Health 1992). Early indications are that the Children Act has led to a decrease in the numbers of children being looked after by local authorities, by agreement or through statutory means, but that there has been less progress in developing initiatives which respond to 'children in need'.

CONCLUSION

In many respects the social worker's role is not an enviable one, the possibilities of progressive practice being hemmed in by the real economic, social, organisational and ideological pressures being experienced by both families and professionals. Perhaps it is also important to recognise the remarkable strengths children and their parents living in adverse circumstances have. Where these strengths can be recognised and 'fostered, developed and sustained' (Stevenson 1992: 31) through the progressive practice of social workers and other professionals working in partnerships with children and parents, then the aims of the Children Act may be realised.

REFERENCES

Bradshaw, Jonathan (1990) *Child Poverty and Deprivation in the UK.* London, National Children's Bureau.

Brown, M. and Madge, N. (1982) *Despite the Welfare State.* London, Heinemann.

Department of Health (1989) *The Care of Children: Principles and Practice in Regulations and Guidance.* London, HMSO.

—— (1991a) *The Children Act 1989, Guidance and Regulations*, Vol. 2; *Family Support, Day Care and Educational Provision for Young Children.* London, HMSO.

—— (1991b) *Working Together.* London, HMSO.

—— (1991c) *Patterns and Outcomes in Child Placement.* London, HMSO.

—— (1992) *Children Act Report.* London, HMSO.

Department of Health and Social Security (1974) *Report of the Committee of Inquiry into the Care and Supervision Provided in Relation to Maria Colwell.* London, HMSO.

—— (1987) *The Law on Child Care and Family Services.* London, HMSO.

Eekelaar, John, and Dingwall, Robert (1990) *The Reform of Child Care Law.* London, Routledge.

Family Rights Group (1991) *The Children Act 1989.* London, HMSO.

Flin, Rhona (1991, 'Sources of stress for child witnesses in court', in K. Murray and D. Gough (1991) *Interviewing in Child Sexual Abuse.* Edinburgh, Scottish Academic Press..

Freeman, Michael (1992) *Children, Their Families, and the Law.* London, Macmillan and BASW.

Gil, David (1970) *Violence Against Children.* Cambridge MA, Harvard University Press.

Gill, Owen (1992) *Parenting Under Pressure.* Cardiff, Barnardo's.

Grimshaw, Roger, and Sumner, Maggie (1991) *What's Happening in Child Care Assessment*. London, National Children's Bureau.

Holman, Robert (1988) *Putting Families First: Prevention and Child Care*. London, Children's Society/Macmillan Education.

Home Office and Department of Health (1992) *Memorandum of Good Practice*. London, HMSO.

London Borough of Brent (1985) *A Child in Trust: Report of the Panel of Inquiry Investigating the Circumstances Surrounding the Death of Jasmine Beckford*. London, Borough of Brent.

London Borough of Greenwich (1987) *A Child in Mind: Protection of Children in a Responsible Society. Report of the Commission of Inquiry Investigating the Circumstances Surrounding the Death of Kimberley Carlile*. London, Borough of Greenwich.

London Borough of Lambeth (1989) *Whose Child? The Report of the Panel Appointed to Inquire into the Death of Tyra Henry*. London, Borough of Lambeth.

Masson, Judith (1992) 'Managing risk under the Children Act 1989: diversion in child care' *Child Abuse Review*, 1, 103–22.

Murray, Kathleen, and Gough, David (1991) *Interviewing in Child Sexual Abuse*. Edinburgh, Scottish Academic Press.

National Children's Homes (1992) *The NCH Factfile: Children in Britain 1992*. London, NCH.

NSPCC/University of Warwick (1993) *Henley Safe Children Interim Report*. Coventry, NSPCC/University of Warwick.

Parton, Nigel (1991) *Governing the Family: Child Care, Child Protection and the State*. London, Macmillan.

Scottish Office (1992) *Report into the Inquiry into the Removal of Children from Orkney in February 1991*. Edinburgh, HMSO.

Secretary of State for Social Services (1988) *Report of the Inquiry into Child Abuse in Cleveland*. London, HMSO.

Shemmings, David (1991) *Client Access to Records: Participation in Social Work*. Aldershot, Avebury.

Stevenson, O. (1992) 'Social work intervention to protect children: aspects of research and practice', *Child Abuse Review*, 1, 19–32.

Wattam, Corinne (1992) *Making a Case in Child Protection*. Harlow, Longman and NSPCC.

Chapter 10

Young children in the care system

Sonia Jackson

The child welfare system in Britain is going through a period of change and reappraisal as fundamental as that which characterised the setting up of the Children's Departments in 1948. The implementation of the Children Act 1989 marked a decisive shift in philosophy from child rescue to family preservation, and this has had more impact on children under 5 than on any other age group. Nevertheless, as I shall argue in this chapter, these youngest and most vulnerable children remain largely invisible within the care system.

Significant changes in ideology, practice and law relating to childcare in Britain have regularly followed incidents or cases that have aroused widespread public concern or indignation, sometimes amounting to 'moral panic' (Jenkins 1992; Black 1992), but often justified by subsequent research or official enquiries. Sometimes the publicity generated may focus political attention on an issue already identified by research or practice. Thus the Curtis Report, which followed the death in foster care of Dennis O'Neill, uncovered a system of substitute care still drawing its view of childhood from the nineteenth-century Poor Law. The Maria Colwell enquiry (DHSS 1974) highlighted the potential conflict between parents' rights and children's welfare which was already the subject of intense debate. Goldstein *et al.* (1973) argued from a theoretical perspective that, at least for young children, the immediate caregivers were more important psychologically than biological parents, and Rowe and Lambert's research (1973) suggested that there were large numbers of children drifting in care who might have been found substitute families if it were easier to dispense with parental consent. Evidence from the National Child Development Study (Seglow 1972) strongly supported the view that adoption was likely to produce the best outcomes for children in care in cases where their parents could not look after them to an acceptable standard.

The 1975 Children Act gave legal expression to these ideas and was very clearly a product of the rescue end of the child welfare spectrum. Children were not to be left in limbo while social workers procrastinated and parents hoped for better times. Firm decisions could be taken in the child's long-term interests even if it meant overriding the wishes of birth families. To many it seemed like common sense to remove children from abusive parents and give them to the many frustrated would-be adopters who would love and care for them. There were others who saw the measures in a wider social policy perspective, and pointed out that with adequate resources not mentioned in the Act, such as housing, work, income support and daycare, most parents would be able to care for their own children (Holman 1980). Holman's argument was later given strong support by a statistical analysis which showed that children in care are overwhelmingly drawn from the most disadvantaged section of the population. Bebbington and Miles (1989) found that predisposing factors for admission to care were a single parent, the household head receiving income support, four or more children, mixed ethnic origin, a privately rented home and one or more persons per room. When all the factors were present the chances of a child coming into care were one in 10, as compared with one in 7,000 for a child of the same age when none of these conditions applied.

THE CARE POPULATION

The concern of those who led the campaign which resulted in the 1975 Act was primarily with young children. Their vision was of a better life for children who would otherwise come into care early and stay long. But already the effects of the Children and Young Persons Act 1969 were changing the character of the care population. Throughout the 1980s the care system became increasingly preoccupied with containing troublesome adolescents, a trend that was set to continue (Parker 1987) and is strongly reflected in current research interests and literature.

In contrast to the 1989 Children Act, the 1975 Act was very sluggishly implemented, and the climate of opinion was changing by the time that many of its provisions came into operation. There was anxiety about the shift from voluntary to compulsory care, from under half in 1962 to over three-quarters of all children in care by 1980 and the increased use of Place of Safety Orders (Packman *et al.* 1986). Meanwhile the American concept of 'permanency planning', aiming to ensure that every child has a chance to grow up in a stable and committed family, was redefined with the emphasis on returning children and maintaining them in their own homes rather than placing them for adoption (Maluccio *et al.* 1986).

By the mid-1980s the number of children in care, which had risen steadily to a peak of over 100,000 in 1978, was on the decline, both absolutely and proportionately, and this trend has accelerated. However, to get an accurate picture of what is happening it is necessary not only to look at the figures of children in care at any one time but also at how long they stay, and that shows that there are two very different groups. Young children are still coming into the care system in quite large numbers, but the great majority return home within a few weeks or months. Older children and adolescents stay longer, and if they are still in care after six months risk spending the remainder of their childhood away from their families (Millham *et al.* 1986; Bullock *et al.* 1993).

In 1991, just before the implementation of the 1989 Children Act, although the overall number of children in care had continued to fall, the figures for children aged 1 to 4 were moving in the opposite direction. Between 1987 and 1991 they rose from 7,900 to 9,100, an increase in the rate per 1,000 population from 3.31 to 3.6 (Department of Health 1991a). However, the Children Act Report 1992 (Department of Health 1993) shows a reversal of this trend. The overall number of children 'looked after' by local authorities was 55,000, compared with 59,800 in care on the same date in 1991, but the largest proportional reduction was in the under-5 age group, from 10,807 to 9,500.

It is worth noting how difficult it is from the published statistics to tease out information about under-fives. However, it can be deduced that a very small proportion, less than 3 per cent, are in residential units, 58 per cent in foster care, and the remainder in unspecified other forms of care, probably either in their own homes or with relatives. Almost all Social Services departments now have a policy of placing children under 10 in foster care if at all possible, so that the majority of the 276 under-fives in community homes on 31 March 1991 may have been in transit or being looked after during some family or foster home crisis.

THE CHANGING CARE SYSTEM

The Children Act 1989 changed the terminology of child welfare as well as its philosophy. Children are no longer in the care of the local authority but 'looked after' or 'accommodated'. The idea of parental rights is replaced by that of parental responsibility, which in the case of a 'looked after' child is shared between the birth parents and the local authority. This change had two objectives: to destigmatise the notion of 'care' and to improve the possibility of working in partnership with parents by minimising the coercive aspects of Social Services intervention. It was intended to encourage parents to ask for help without fear that they would thereby lose all control and influence over their children's lives, as often happened in the past (Millham *et al.* 1986). The intention was that court orders should be used only when they were essential for the child's protection.

There has already been a very marked drop in the number of care orders (Department of Health 1993) and Emergency Protection Orders are running at a far lower level than the Place of Safety Orders which they replaced. Even more important is the change in attitudes and practice of social workers, of which this is the most visible sign. Young children are particularly affected because of their greater vulnerability, which in the past made social workers more anxious to use legal means to assert their authority. This is understandable in the light of the long series of child abuse reports which regularly concluded with searing criticisms of social workers (Reder *et al.* 1993). However, Packman *et al.* (1986) showed that Place of Safety Orders were regularly being used in situations where there was neither an emergency nor a high level of risk.

The extended period between the passage of the Children Act in 1989 and its implementation in October 1991, during which intensive training took place in all local authorities, provided an opportunity to observe social work practice in transition. Marian Brandon carried out a detailed analysis of seven cases from different local authorities, six of them involving children under 5, from which she concluded that both the philosophy and legal requirements of the Act had the potential to change practice significantly (Brandon 1992). In most cases a much higher level of compulsion was exerted than necessary, the potential and willingness to help of family members other than the mother was overlooked, and assessment took precedence over support. Workers were aware of the need to change but had not yet incorporated this into their everyday practice. This small study usefully indicates the fundamental changes in attitude that will be necessary if the idea of partnership with families, so central to the Children Act, is to be realised.

SUPPORTING PARENTS

A further argument for blurring the boundaries of the care system comes from research which shows how unclear was the distinction in the past between children who were received into care and those who remained at home. Jean Packman found little difference in the situation and needs of children in care and a comparison group of children in contact with social services (Packman *et al.* 1986). In fact children, mostly the younger ones, who had been abused or neglected (her 'victims' category), were rather less likely to come into care than older children with troublesome behaviour (the 'villains'), but they did not necessarily receive a high level of social work support at home. A great deal depended on the ethos of the social services team and the particular social worker involved.

Redefining care, or accommodation, as a form of support for families in difficulties rather than a last resort, could mean that the service is more accurately matched to the children's needs. Short-term foster care has always been used in this way, but with increased emphasis on parental responsibility and contact, the way is opened for the system of respite care, so successful in helping families of children with disabilities, to be more widely used to support other parents who have difficulty in caring for their children without periods of relief. There are obvious attractions in such a policy, but the problems of transferring the scheme to a different client group have not really been addressed.

The changes highlight an aspect of care that has received little attention until recently: the experience of returning home. We know that return after a period of separation is likely to be problematic for very young children, who on reunion with the absent parent often react with hostility or being excessively demanding (Bowlby 1953). These difficulties are likely to be compounded by the fact that children in care usually come from families with a membership which is 'fluid and volatile' as well as geographically mobile (Bullock *et al.* 1993). Thus the child may be returning to a different place and a different set of relationships from those she left. Step-parents or stepbrothers and -sisters may find it particularly hard to understand and tolerate the disturbed behaviour which, after a brief honeymoon period, often follows return (Bullock *et al.* 1993). There may be the additional stress of being supplanted by a new baby.

There are several indications from this study and others that there are special factors affecting the youngest children. Farmer and Parker's (1991) research on children 'home on trial' found that success was strongly age-related. However, in common with almost all research on childcare, there is no particular focus in this study on under-fives, and the form of the analysis does not make it possible to discuss the findings specifically in relation to this age-group. We know that most of these young children are in care for a relatively short time on any one occasion. However, returning home cannot be equated with a good outcome for the child. For example, in the Farmer and Parker study, 42 of 172 children who were in care primarily for protection were reabused or neglected in their 'home on trial' placement. The fact that only nine of these children were removed again may reflect the reluctance of social workers to admit failure rather than the quality of the children's lives. Moreover, we do not know what proportion of children who experience repeated short-term admissions in their early years re-enter the care system later as problem adolescents.

FOSTER CARE AND ADOPTION

With the swing of the pendulum away from child rescue to family preservation, adoption has fallen increasingly out of fashion as a form of substitute care. Paradoxically, social workers may be more inclined to consider adoption for 'hard to place' children than for those with fewer difficulties. An analysis of 10,000 placements in six local authorities involving 5,688 children (Rowe *et al.* 1989) found that only 2 per cent were adopted.

Research in progress suggests that social workers generally regard long-term foster care as an acceptable 'permanent placement' even when the child has little or no contact with the natural family and no realistic prospect of reunion. Sadly, many apparently satisfactory foster homes break down when the child's care becomes less straightforward, as in adolescence, or for reasons unconnected with the child – illness, divorce, even moving house. Furthermore, research on young people leaving care suggests that, unlike birth or adoptive families, foster carers do not make a commitment guaranteed to last into adulthood (Biehal *et al.* 1992). At the time of writing, adoption law is once more under review, but the outcome is likely to confirm the trend towards more open adoption, transferring parental responsibility without necessarily severing all links with the child's family of origin. This could reduce obstacles to adoption in some cases.

Although the emphasis in the Children Act on supporting families to provide care for their own children is very welcome, it carries a risk of encouraging unrealistic optimism. The result may be that many young children who could be sucessfully adopted have their early development stunted, perhaps irrevocably, by care of a barely acceptable level, or by frequent movement between placements. If we take seriously the Children Act principle that the welfare of the child is paramount, social workers should consider adoption much more often and at an earlier stage than they currently do.

The quality of foster care

Foster care is likely to remain the placement of choice for most young children, with the aim of returning them to their families as soon as possible. What is their experience? Again, this is a subject on which we have little firm information. Most research, as well as most practice related to fostering, has been about placement and whether it lasts or breaks down rather than what happens to the child within the foster home. Indeed, once foster parents have been approved, after an assessment process which has become increasingly elaborate and exhaustive, their treatment of the child within their own home has taken on some of the privacy which is normally accorded to family life.

However, perceptions of fostering were undergoing significant changes well before the Children Act. An important conceptual distinction has been made between 'exclusive' fostering, in which the foster carers aim to replace the birth parents in a quasi-adoptive relationship with the child, and 'inclusive' fostering, where continued contact with the child's birth family is emphasised. Rather contrary to expectations (and in conflict with the position of Goldstein *et al.* 1973), research has consistently shown that foster placements are less likely to break down when natural parents are actively encouraged to visit and maintain their relationship with the child (Berridge and Cleaver 1987). Since these parents are by definition people who have encountered severe difficulties in their lives and have suffered the further blow to their self-concept of failing to provide good enough care for the child, they will not always be easy to deal with. The task of fostering has thus become very complex compared with the days when foster parents were expected to be kind people who would simply take children into their home and care for them 'as if they were their own'.

Although this is recognised in selection and preparation for fostering, and by the increasing use of the term 'foster carer' in place of 'foster parent', it seems to have made much less impact on the monitoring and support of foster care once a child has been placed. Statutory visits can often be perfunctory affairs, with no clear agenda. At worst this raises the concern that much undetected abuse may occur in foster homes, a subject already intensely discussed in North America but which still simmers below the surface here. The possibility is one we do not want to entertain – as was evident in the press build-up to the Cleveland Enquiry, when the paediatricians' finding that a child had been further abused by a foster father was regarded as convincing evidence that the doctors and social workers were obsessed and deluded.

However, leaving aside the possibility of abuse, there are many unanswered questions about the quality of foster care for very young children. Foster carers are in short supply, and the overriding concern of social workers has inevitably been with placement. The child development element in social work training has been progressively eroded as more and more has to be fitted into a two-year programme. As a result social workers may have little specialist knowledge of young children and assume (usually correctly) that the foster carer knows better than they do how to meet the child's needs. Add to that the fact that most placements of young children are for short periods, and the weaknesses in support and monitoring of this age-group are easily understood.

A new initiative, based at the University of Bristol and

supported by the Department of Health, is attempting to address this problem. The research team has developed and is currently evaluating a comprehensive scheme designed to assess the outcomes of child welfare interventions and feed them immediately back into practice. The core of the Looking After Children scheme, described in detail in the book of the same name (Parker *et al.* 1991) is a set of Assessment and Action Records for children of different ages.

The concept of outcome is broken down into seven dimensions: health, education, identity, social and family relationships, emotional and behavioural development, social presentation and, except for babies under one year, self-care skills. All these are areas of concern to parents looking after their own children. The idea is that local authorities, undertaking the corporate parenting of a child, should set themselves the same aims and ensure that the necessary actions are taken to achieve them as would a 'reasonable' parent of a child of the same age.

In the case of a separated child under 5 placed with foster carers, this implies much closer scrutiny and more detailed discussion with foster carers than would usually have occurred in the past.

Take, for example, Alison, a 3-year-old placed with her younger brother Jason in a short-term foster home while her single mother was recovering in hospital from a severe depressive illness. The children were expected to be looked after for a minimum of nine months. The first consequence of the scheme was that Alison's developmental needs were looked at individually, apart from those of her brother. In planning for the four months review required under the Children Act, the social worker, foster carers and Alison's grandmother, in the course of several meetings, reviewed each developmental dimension and decided what action, if any, needed to be taken. In the process of these discussions the roles of the participants were clarified and enhanced. For instance the foster mother had not liked to suggest that Alison attend a playgroup because she felt she was being paid to care for her full time (the social worker was able to reassure her). She was also concerned about Alison's constant demands for 'sweeties' and whether it was right to refuse them. Alison had magazines to look at in the foster home but her carers assumed she was too young for proper books. As a result of discussion on this point it was agreed that Alison's grandmother would visit each week to take her to the children's library, achieving a three-way objective of giving her attention apart from Jason, maintaining family contact, and introducing the idea of books as a source of interest and pleasure.

Giving the grandmother an active role also proved important in relation to Alison's developing sense of identity, a dimension often overlooked in the care of young children. The grandmother and foster parents began to make life-story books for Alison and Jason, recording information that might otherwise have been lost. The children's father was black, but all the other people involved in their care were white. The Assessment and Action Record for 3–4-year-olds asks: 'Is the child aware of her ethnic background?' 'Does she have contact with other adults/children who come from the same ethnic background?' This enabled the social worker to discuss with the carers the importance of enabling children of mixed parentage to develop a positive view of their colour and ethnicity, not an issue which the foster family had previously considered. On the other hand the social worker became more aware of the excellent care which the children were receiving, and was encouraged to acknowledge this explicitly.

The active or compensatory approach to foster care which underpins the Looking After Children scheme is not uncontroversial. It has been suggested by social work managers that there are values and practices embedded in the scheme which may result in greater differentiation between the child's family of origin and the foster home placement than would otherwise be the case. However, we need to take into account that children separated from their families are greatly disadvantaged in ways we are only beginning to understand. An Oxford University study of the educational progress of children aged 9–13 in stable foster care showed them performing well below average at school even when they had been in the same foster home since early childhood (Heath *et al.* 1989). Those who had been abused or neglected were especially likely to have low educational attainment. The conclusion of the researchers was that if you place children with exceptional needs in average families, you only get average progress, that is, not enough to make up for earlier deficits (Jackson 1992). This is a clear argument for a strong focus on education or cognitive development in the earliest years when we know so much learning takes place (Sylva and Moss 1992). Of course it applies equally to children 'in need' when family support is provided through daycare.

CHILD WELFARE AND DAYCARE

Family support, childcare for working parents, preschool education and substitute care for separated children are usually discussed as if they were entirely separate matters. The Children Act 1989 does for the first time in any piece of legislation, encompass them all, but in separate sections and volumes of Guidance and Regulations (Department of Health 1991b). Of course they are intimately related, especially for children under school age. As already indicated, poverty and isolation are the main underlying reasons why young children cannot be cared for within their own families. Maternal depression and mental illness, which often contribute to neglect and ill-treatment, have been shown repeatedly to be associated with unrelieved care of young children. It is clear then that the failure of successive British governments to develop a coherent policy for the care and education of children under 5, especially affordable good-quality daycare, is responsible to a large extent for the creation of the 'need' that local authorities with their restricted budgets are expected to meet. In countries which have better levels of family support, which acknowledge the financial costs of childrearing, which protect the rights of parents in their employment laws and allocate resources to children as an investment in the future, the need for substitute childcare is minuscule by comparison with ours. It is significant that, leaving aside Eastern Europe, the only country where the need for substitute care is increasing is in the United States, which like us has failed to tackle the related problems of family poverty and affordable daycare (National Commission on Foster Family Care 1991).

However, daycare in this country does play a crucially important role on the fringes of the 'looked after' system. It is the only effective resource available to social workers when there are serious doubts about a family's capacity to care for a child. Very little detailed guidance is available either to social workers or nursery workers about how they can collaborate effectively in this situation. There is a tendency for social workers to hand over to the nursery and reduce contact with the parents instead of planning together how they can support and help the child and family and at the same time acknowledge their separate contributions and responsibilities (Goldschmied and Jackson 1993). For example, it is the nursery workers' task to offer the child sensitive care and satisfying educational experiences, the social worker's to arrange for reconnection of the electricity supply, without which the parent cannot provide satisfactory physical care. If the Children Act does achieve its aim of making accommodation just one of many ways of supporting families, collaboration between Social Services childcare teams, foster carers and the other systems relating to under-fives – nursery schools and classes, day nurseries, family centres, childminders, playgroups and home visiting schemes – will become increasingly vital.

CONCLUSION

This chapter has explored the changes occurring in our child welfare system, particularly as a result of the Children Act 1989 and the different expectations of social workers and carers which it has produced. However, although under-fives make up a significant proportion of the 'looked after' population, their particular needs and characteristics have received little attention. There is an urgent need for further research focusing specifically on this age group.

One important issue that has not been discussed in this chapter because as yet its impact has hardly been felt, is the government's determination to promote private and voluntary organisations as providers of services, reducing the local authority's role to that of purchaser. So far this policy has been most actively pursued in relation to health care and community care for older people, and as the only form of expansion envisaged in daycare for working parents. If the purchaser-provider split became widespread in childcare it would be likely to result in acute conflicts for social workers and carers, as it has in the United States, with financial considerations increasingly taking precedence over the well-being of children. Research over the past ten years, taken forward by the 1989 Children Act, and its associated guidance and initiatives, has produced significant improvements in the services offered to young children in need. There is a high risk that unless child welfare professionals and carers inform themselves of the policy issues and adopt an active campaigning position, all these advances may go into reverse.

REFERENCES

Bebbington, A. and Miles, J. (1989) 'The background of children who enter local authority care', *British Journal of Social Work*, 19, 5.

Berridge, D. (1985) *Children's Homes*. Oxford, Blackwell.

Berridge, D. and Cleaver, H. (1987) *Foster Home Breakdown*. Oxford, Blackwell.

Biehal, N., Clayden, J., Stein, M. and Wade, J. (1992) *Prepared for Living? A Survey of Young People Leaving the Care of Three Local Authorities*. London, National Children's Bureau.

Black, R. (1992) *Orkney: a Place of Safety?* Edinburgh, Canongate Press.

Bowlby, J. (1953) *Child Care and the Growth of Love*. Harmondsworth, Penguin.

Brandon, M. (1992) 'Anticipating the impact of the Children Act on social work practice in child care', *Adoption and Fostering*, 16, 2.

Bullock, R., Little, M. and Millham, S. (1993) *Going Home: The Return of Children Separated from their Families*. Aldershot, Dartmouth.

Department of Health (1991a) *Patterns and Outcomes in Child Placement*. London, HMSO.

—— (1991b) *The Children Act 1989, Guidance and Regulations*, Vols 2 and 3. London, HMSO.

—— (1993) *Children Act Report*. London, HMSO.

DHSS (1974) *Report of the Committee of Inquiry into the Care and Supervision Provided in Relation to Maria Colwell*. London, HMSO.

Farmer, E. and Parker, R.A. (1991) *Trials and Tribulations*. London, HMSO.

Goldschmied, E. and Jackson, S. (1993) *People Under Three*. London, Routledge.

Goldstein, J., Freud, A. and Solnit, A.J. (1973) *Beyond the Best Interests of the Child*. London, Free Press.

Heath, A., Colton, M. and Aldgate, J. (1989) 'The education of children in care', *British Journal of Social Work*, 19, 447–60.

Holman, R. (1980) *Inequality in Child Care*. London, Child Poverty Action Group.

Jackson, S. (1987) *The Education of Children in Care*. Bristol Papers in Applied Social Studies, No. 1, University of Bristol.

—— (1992) *The Education of Children in Need*, Report of a Seminar held at the Department of Social Work, University of Bristol, 30 September.

Jenkins, P. (1992) *Intimate Enemies: Moral Panics in Contemporary Great Britain*. New York, Aldine de Gruyter.

London Borough of Brent (1985) *A Child in Trust, The Report of the Panel of Inquiry into the Circumstances Surrounding the Death of Jasmine Beckford*. London, Kingswood Press.

Maluccio, A.N., Fein, E. and Olmstead, K.A. (1986) *Permanency Planning for Children: Concepts and Methods*. London, Routledge & Kegan Paul.

Millham, S., Bullock, R., Hosie, K. and Haak, M. (1986) *Lost in Care: The Problems of Maintaining Links Between Children in Care and their Families*. Aldershot, Gower.

National Commission on Foster Family Care (1991) *A Blueprint for Fostering Infants, Children and Youth in the 1990s*. Washington, Child Welfare League of America.

Packman, J., Randall, J. and Jacques, N. (1986) *Who Needs Care?*. Oxford, Blackwell.

Parker, R.A. (1987) *Residential Care: Australian Lessons for Britain*. Aldershot, Gower.

Parker, R.A., Ward, H., Jackson, S., Aldgate, J. and Wedge, P. (eds) (1991) *Looking After Children: Outcomes in Child Care*. London, HMSO.

Reder, P., Duncan, S. and Gray, M. (1993) *Beyond Blame: Child Abuse Tragedies Revisited*. London, Routledge.

Rowe, J. and Lambert, L. (1973) *Children Who Wait*. London, Association of British Adoption Agencies.

Rowe, J., Hundleby, M. and Garnett, L. (1989) *Child Care Now*. London, BAAF.

Seglow, J., Pringle, M.K. and Wedge, P. (1972) *Growing Up Adopted*. Slough, National Foundation for Educational Research.

Sylva, K. and Moss, P. (1992) *Learning Before School*. National Commission on Education Briefing No. 8. London, NCE.

Chapter 11

Making a difference for children 'in need'
'Educare' services

Tricia David

The previous chapters explored some of the contexts in which children may be deemed 'in need' according to the criteria delineated in the Children Act 1989.

In this chapter I intend to explore the ways in which families can be supported by the provision of early childhood services, but also to challenge the idea that it is only children in particularly disadvantaged circumstances who should have access to these.

The Health Visitors' Association carried out a survey at the time the Children Act was being implemented (in 1991), and discovered to their dismay that many health visitors were defining as 'in need' only those children who were identifiable as having severe learning difficulties. Health visitors and other professionals, for example social workers, probation officers, education welfare officers and GPs, have traditionally maintained contact with local authority nurseries and playgroups. They can sometimes recommend to families that their young children need the opportunities these nurseries and playgroups offer, and that sometimes the parents themselves need either respite from childcare, or the opportunities groups can offer parents through networking, and so on.

What specifically are thought to be the benefits for the children in such circumstances?

CHILDREN WITH LEARNING DIFFICULTIES

Children with special needs are thought to benefit from early experience in a group context in a variety of ways. Firstly, qualified staff may provide important diagnostic assessments which can lead to early intervention, but intervention which seeks to be positive, avoiding the problems of early labelling. This view was recently endorsed by the support for nursery eduction by the Special Needs Consortium in their challenges to the government over the 1993 Education Act, which omitted serious consideration of the future of nursery education. Secondly, by attending a local nursery or playgroup young children with learning difficulties may demonstrate, in a familiar setting, that they would be capable of becoming well integrated into their local 'ordinary' school, ideally with support (if need be), and they will then move on into that context with ready-made friends. Having friends you can play with in your neighbourhood can also be an important, developmentally beneficial factor. Thirdly, parents of children with learning difficulties have often found that not only were their children isolated, but so were they themselves (see Chapter 7). However, parents of children with special needs, whether these are Baroness Warnock's (DES 1978) 2 per cent, or the one child in five who may at some time during their lives have some form of learning difficulty, may fear that their child will not be welcome in a nursery group because they will be overly demanding on staff time, or that they may disrupt the play and learning of other children. This means that we need to ensure staff have appropriate training, that adult:child ratios are also appropriate, and that other parents understand the ways in which their children benefit too from the comprehensive nature of such provision.

SIGNIFICANT HARM

As Norma Baldwin and Chris Harrison have pointed out (Chapter 9), the new concept of 'significant harm' may, like the concept of 'in need', be subject to differing interpretations. Both concepts may be translated into action by professionals and volunteers according to the resources known to be available, rather than according to clearly defined criteria relating to children whose life situation is in some way threatening their development, emotionally, physically or socially. As Professor Ron Davie, former director of the National Children's Bureau, has said (personal communication), 'Parliament has moved the landing strip and some in the child protection services have not realised this yet'.

Nursery provision has been one of the traditional ways in which social workers and other professionals have sought to alleviate the stress in the lives of families, especially where they were afraid children could be at risk of injury or abuse if left day after day in such circumstances. In the past this has sometimes meant services were seen as 'rescue' for the children, or as offering 'compensatory educational input' for children from homes where poverty was interpreted as 'social or cultural disadvantage'. We know from more recent studies of children at home (e.g. Shinman 1981; Davie *et al.* 1984; Tizard and Hughes 1984) that it is often lack of confidence in the face of the task of parenting, especially when one compares oneself with trained, experienced, middle-class professionals, that causes parents to appear inept. We know also that most parents provide their children with challenging conversation and are highly capable of stimulating their children's development, given appropriate support and the knowledge to which others have access, but which they may lack. Despite the faith of different professionals in the abilities of nurseries to protect children, we cannot *prove* that the provision of services which are flexible amalgams of education and care for children, support and partnership for parents, can prevent children being neglected or harmed, because to date there have been few studies setting out to explore the effects of preschool early childhood services on prevention. However, the few projects so far attempted seem to point to this as a significant resource in our society (see, for example, Ferri and Saunders 1991; Gibbons *et al.* 1990). As I will explain later, however, it would be preferable if the services were open access, not limited to families with difficulties.

In her chapter on children in care, Sonia Jackson (Chapter 10) draws attention to the discrepancies in achievement among children who have been, or are, in care, compared with children living with their own parents. It may be, of course, that emotional causes underlie this underachievement, but this must not be allowed to be an excuse for ignoring the ways in which children are being failed by the system because workers from one field are not liaising appropriately with those from another. Educare services, combining high-quality care and education, can help by ensuring that children are offered, early in their lives, ways of developing their learning patterns, the expectation that they will achieve, and an understanding of what is expected of them. Margy Whalley (Chapter 12) provides some insights into the lag in professional development which may result in nursery workers having reduced expectations of children whose lives are currently in crisis. Naturally it is important to be sensitive to individual children's needs, but it is also important to ensure they are appropriately stimulated, and it is through observation and monitoring of the child's progress, as advised in the 'Rumbold Report' (DES 1990), that this can be done.

EQUAL OPPORTUNITIES: ISSUES OF LANGUAGE, RACE AND GENDER

The Children Act and the subsequent guidelines (DoH 1991) for implementation stress the importance of positive action in respect of home language, and racist and sexist discrimination in children's lives. To argue that children subjected to these forms of discrimination should come under the umbrella of children 'in need' seems a logical step, if to do so means one must explore the possibility that these children are in some way having their development inhibited. The issue here then is, how do effective early childhood services ensure that children are not suffering from discriminatory policies or practices, and how should services engage with these injustices?

We know that children in their earliest years learn best in their home language, so the recruitment of more educators from ethnic and linguistic minorities is important, as is partnership with parents and communities. If children aged 7 achieved higher SATs scores when their home language was used in the maths and science assessments (Knight 1993), the power of using home language with children under 5 at a time when they are developing their most basic concepts, as well as their under-standings about learning, seems obvious. It is also supported by Vygotsky's (1978) theory of children's learning being social. All providers need to evaluate not only policies, but practices in relation to equal opportunities – it is the ability to develop an awareness of social justice which is probably the most crucial factor, and an ability to observe events, some of them very subtle, in one's workplace to reflect on ways in which staff may have encouraged, even unwittingly, the perpetuation of racism and sexism. For example, one research student at a group where staff avowed commitment to equal opportunities observed the ways in which 'white children' would gradually take over the most prominent positions relative to a worker, would supplant a 'black child' on the worker's lap, without the worker becoming aware of what had happened, how she had colluded in this process, or the ultimate implications in terms of the hidden curriculum. We know that this is similar to the evidence (French and French 1984) about boys' behaviour in primary classrooms.

QUALITY OF PROVISION

Part III of the Children Act 1989 details legal requirements to be made of local authorities in respect of support for children and their families. These requirements include a general duty to

> safeguard and promote the welfare of children within their area who are in need; and ... to promote the upbringing of such children by their families.
>
> (Children Act 1989, Part III: 17)

Local authorities are expected to facilitate the provision of daycare services 'as is appropriate', for children in need, who are under 5 but who do not yet attend schools. The Act also suggests that local authorities may provide such facilities for children under 5 who are not deemed to be 'in need', but whatever services are offered, they should be reviewed triennially, jointly by the Social Services and education departments.

In the guidelines issued (DoH 1991) to support the implementation of the Children Act, the main factors said to influence the quality of care are as follows:

- the nature of adult–child interaction;
- the nature of the interaction between children/peers;
- size of group and numbers of staff;
- continuity, training and experience of staff;
- recognition of children's developmental needs;
- type of contract/involvement between parent and provider;
- ability to support and structure children's learning;
- elements in programme of activities;
- equality of opportunity policy in employment and service delivery;
- children's involvement in planning and choosing activities and projects;
- elements of imagination, challenge and adventure in activities;
- organisation, display and accessibility of equipment, toys and materials;
- attention to health, safety and type of physical environment.

'Defining quality of care involves looking at these factors from the point of view of child development as well as the rights or expectations of children, parents and people with young children' (DoH 1991: paras 6.25, 6.26).

The guidelines stress further the importance of care which is developmentally beneficial to the child, compared with 'poor quality care' which is said to inhibit, or at least not facilitate, child development.

Thus we see quite clearly that all services for young children are expected to have developmentally beneficial effects, and, in particular, that they should provide planned opportunities for learning.

In addition to the above criteria, the European Childcare Network has suggested that services need to be accessible and flexible, according to families' needs, that the views of parents should be taken into account, and that provision should reflect the local community, and that it should be cost effective. Both the EC Childcare Network (1992) and the Rumbold Committee have stressed the need for central government policies and legislation. Leaving the responsibility to local authorities in the past has led to the muddle and unfairness which constantly dogs this sector (Pugh 1992). We have yet to see a local authority taken to court for failing to provide services for the education and care of young children, but it may come to that. The European Community issued a Recommendation in March 1992 (Cohen 1993) requesting action in four areas:

> services for children; leave arrangements for parents; making the environment, structure and organisation of work responsive to the needs of workers with children; promoting the sharing of responsibilities for children between women and men.
>
> (Cohen 1993: 11)

One of the articles of this Recommendation requires member states to inform the European Commission by 1995, of action taken.

Children in the UK are among those for whom there is least provision compared with other EC countries. Perhaps one could argue that this means there are a great many children 'in need', because their needs may not be being met appropriately by this lack of services. For example, some families are cutting down on the number of playgroup sessions attended by their children because they are in financial difficulties; some parents (i.e. this usually means mothers) who go out to work are having to place their children in more than one form of provision in order to cover their work hours; some may simply be unable to get a place for a child who desperately needs the experience of being with other children. The most acute lack in provision in this country affects children under 2, and while Judy Warner (Chapter 3) has provided a powerful case for childminding, and while this may indeed be the most popular form of provision numerically, and may have greatly improved its image and performance, research indicates that many parents would like the possibility of choosing group provision (Bone 1977; David 1992), perhaps because they want their child's horizons widened through group experience. Vivienne Whittingham (Chapter 6) adds that some private providers feel that free local authority places in nursery schools and classes rob them of their 3-year-olds, and many playgroup supervisors may well feel the same when their 'older children' are similarly removed by parents expecting not only the free place, but the expertise of qualified teachers and nursery nurses, before their children embark on the National Curriculum. Searching for more positive solutions for the benefit of the children, and for their parents and staff seems to be the answer. Expecting our youngest children to thrive when being moved on from one setting to another at this crucial time in their development seems like profligacy with our most valuable assets.

CONCLUSIONS

Many local authorities (see Chapter 14) are making bold attempts to provide sensitive and sensible services for all their children. It seems obvious, but research now bears out the fact (Cochran 1986), that it is better to have local services which involve all families in a neighbourhood who wish to be involved, rather than services which become labelled as 'rescue', in turn, labelling the children and parents who use them, and which at the same time exclude other families.

How this might be achieved without some form of central government lead and policies is somewhat tricky. One model which appears feasible is that based on a Danish system, where parents do make some contributions to costs, but children may stay at the one form of provision throughout the early years. The service is intended to be flexible and child-centred. (Although Audrey Curtis, in Chapter 13, draws attention to the levels of training of educators in Denmark compared with current teacher education in the UK, this is one qualification the Danish government is developing to degree level.) This model might better facilitate the exchange of expertise between providers, for it is largely as a result of history and past policies in the UK that differences between educators still impinge on their attempts to cooperate. Mistrust and differences in aims and focus do not make for strong links and mutual understanding in what has become a multi-professional field in its own right. Unfortunately some of the new 'market approach' education legislation does not help foster a climate of sharing. While nursery teachers have much to offer colleagues in the voluntary and private sectors in terms of providing for children's learning, they are now being expected to charge for this, and quite naturally the voluntary and private providers are asking where such fees will come from. Equally, teachers, many of whom may have traditionally focused on children's learning, would probably be the first to admit their need for training and support in developing their work with parents, and colleagues from the social services day nursery sector, combined centres, and playgroups have much to offer here.

Perhaps in this country the way forward would be to emulate the service provided by combined nursery/family centres, which are still very few and have generally been placed in areas of disadvantage. Combinations of locally provided facilities, which coordinate their services are needed so that childminders and group provision become part of a network, and the expertise of each educator could be appropriately valued. This model seems the closest we may come, in the present climate, to true 'educare' and partnership with parents, by building on existing provision as necessary, so that no provider need feel under threat – the quickest way to destroy collaboration. A climate which recognised the strengths of providers and the loyalty and commitment of the parents who use their service, by ensuring adequate funding, provision for high-quality training, improved conditions and status of staff would be reflected in the experiences of the children.

Staff at Childline have reported that when children ring them one of their strategies is to ask the children to think and talk about a time when they were happy. One of the most frequently cited is 'when I went to nursery/playgroup' (James 1993). It always seems sad that preschool services have constantly to prove their long-term effectiveness, and usually this is measured in terms of children's later school achievements. We know that early group experience that is educational/high quality makes a difference (e.g. see Melhuish and Moss 1991; Shorrocks 1992), although there will be critics who say 'free, maintained nursery education does not make a difference to children from homes which are not disadvantaged'. But how can we know when few such children have had the opportunity to attend other than a playgroup? We suspect that children's moral development may also be enhanced by early education, certainly Russian researchers would suggest this (OMEP/UNESCO 1993). Perhaps one of the most powerful arguments for group provision is the increasing isolation of families with young children, and their need to feel support is available within their own community.

The question then seems to be 'can we afford *not* to provide educare services for children and their families, whether they are defined as "in need" or not?'

REFERENCES

Bone, M. (1977) *Preschool Children and the Need for Daycare*. London, HMSO.

Cochran, M. (1986) 'The parental empowerment process building on family strengths', in J.Harris (ed.) *Child Psychology in Action*. London, Croom Helm.

Cohen, B. (1993) 'A programme for Europe', *Child Education*, 70, 2, 11.

David, T. (1992) 'What do parents want their children to learn in preschool in Belgium and the UK?' Paper presented at the XXth International OMEP World Congress, NAU, USA, August 1992.

Davie, C., Hutt, S.J., Vincent, E. and Mason, M. (1984) *The Young Child at Home*. Windsor, NFER-Nelson.

DES (1978) *Report of the Committee of Enquiry into the Education of Handicapped Children and Young People* (Warnock Report). London, HMSO.

—— (1990) *Starting with Quality* (Rumbold Report). London, HMSO.

DoH (1991) *The Children Act 1989. Guidance and Regulations Volume 2 Family Support, Day Care and Educational Provision for Young Children.* London, HMSO.

EC Childcare Network (1992) *Quality of Services for Young Children*. Brussels, European Commission.

Ferri, E. and Saunders, A. (1991) *Parents, Professionals and Pre-school Centres*. London, NCB/Barnardo's.

French, J. and French, P. (1984) 'Gender imbalance in primary classrooms', *Educational Research*, 26, 2.

Gibbons, J., Thorpe, S. and Wilkinson, P. (1990) *Family Support and Prevention: Studies in Local Areas*. London, HMSO.

House of Commons (1989) *The Children Act 1989*. London, HMSO.

James, C. (1993) 'Striking the balance', Paper presented to the East Hertfordshire Nursery, Infant and First Schools' Headteachers' Conference, Hertford, February 1993.

Knight, C. (1993) 'Nursery experience, home language and the SATs', *OMEP Update*, 55, 1–2.

Melhuish, E. and Moss, P. (1991) *Day Care for Young Children*. London, Routledge.

OMEP/UNESCO (1993) *The Universal and the National in Preschool Education*. Paris, UNESCO.

Pugh, G. (ed.) (1992) *Contemporary Issues in the Early Years*. London, Paul Chapman/NCB.

Shinman, S. (1981) *A Chance for Every Child*. London, Tavistock.

Shorrocks, D. (1992) 'Evaluating Key Stage I assessments: the testing time of May 1991', *Early Years*, 13, 1, 16–20.

Tizard, B. and Hughes, M. (1984) *Young Children Learning*. London, Fontana.

Vygotsky, L. (1978) *Mind in Society*. Cambridge, MA, Harvard University Press.

Part III

Issues and implications

Chapter 12

Young children in day nurseries and combined centres run by the Social Services department – practitioner research

Margy Whalley

The views presented are those of the author. The research in this chapter was first described in a dissertation submitted as part of an MA in Professional Studies, University of Leicester.

BACKGROUND TO THE RESEACH

In 1987 I took some 'time-out' from the combined, education-social services-health, multi-disciplinary centre for under-fives and families where I work, to reflect on my own practice and to undertake some action research in other early-years establishments. Colin Fletcher (1991) makes the point that there is a 'right time' for practitioner research, and this was my 'right time'.

I was interested in the interface between nursery education, which aims to 'promote' the education of young children, and Social Services daycare provision, which aims at 'preventing' the reception of young children into care. As an early childhood educator with twenty years' experience in education, daycare and community social work settings, I felt that sometimes teachers and day nursery staff did not make the connections between the educational, and the social, emotional and physical care needs of our youngest children.

An ideological rift

Despite the statement by the House of Commons Select Committee in 1990 that 'Care and Education for the Under Fives are complementary and inseparable', it seemed to me that there was a huge philosophical rift between policy-makers at the Department of Education and the Department of Social Services.

The rift appears even wider among senior managers within local government departments where a decade of cost cutting and ever-tighter budgetary control has resulted in even tighter demarcation lines as to where responsibility for children under 5 actually lies. My previous experience setting up and working in early years provisions in Brazil and Papua New Guinea had taught me that ministries and local government could ill afford to separate the education and care needs of children. My recent experience in visiting daycare settings in Northern Italy showed me a new vision of quality edu-care as the right of *every* child.

The history of education and care services

In this country the government seems to have a very ambivalent attitude towards daycare and nursery education. Historically, both nursery education and daycare were linked in that both adopted a compensatory model of working with families which had overtones of 'rescuing'. Only for brief periods during the war years did government departments join together to cater for children from birth to 5 years (Webb 1991; David 1990). Even then there were huge ideological gaps between 'nurses and nannies' who cared for children, and 'teachers' who educated them.

Ideological pressures and economic pressures within a few years of the Second World War reversed thinking about day nurseries 'as a potential preschool resource for all children to one where there is a financial, social or medical reason to necessitate admission' (Van der Eyken 1984; Riley 1983; Fox-Harding 1991).

The daycare settings

I was able to spend a term observing in an experimental combined under-fives provision where an education nursery unit and a Social Services day nursery were sharing one site. This new hybrid under-fives centre seemed to me to represent all the anomalies within both typologies of service provision, i.e. education and care. Here the rhetoric, and reality of the 1960s–80s education model of 'partnership with parents', and the Social Services' 1970s–80s model of 'shared-care' and 'working with families' could be seen and studied in sharp contrast.

Reason and Marshall (1986) argue the case that 'researchers

often choose (awarely or unawarely) research topics which will re-stimulate old patterns of distress'. I became aware that I was most concerned with the powerlessness that staff, parents and children were expressing in the daycare setting. As an early years practitioner with a strong community education background I believe children and adults need to feel in control of their own lives and need to have choices. 'An individual's being is affirmed by and arises out of their choices' (Reason and Marshall 1986). The daycare services which I observed reflected a model of 'control' rather than cooperation (Condry 1986). They were run at an organisational level by women and yet were managed at a strategic level by men on a traditional hierarchical model. Local people were not consulted about the nature of services nor were parents using the services represented at a management level. (Day nurseries, unlike education nurseries, have no governing bodies.) It seemed to me that a service with such a structure was unlikely to empower either users or providers.

The limitation of the research

It is not my intention in this chapter to make sweeping general-isations about local authority daycare from one small in-depth study. Comprehensive research has been undertaken both in the quantity and quality of the limited services that are available in this country (Moss and Melhuish 1991; Marshall 1982; Bain and Barnett 1980).

I do believe, however, that it is both possible and probable that many of the key issues facing daycare workers in the centre I studied in depth are common to other local authority day nurseries. In this chapter I want to tease out some of the contradictions that I found within a particular model of daycare which I believe seriously limits what it can offer to children and to their parents.

CHANGES IN DAY NURSERY PROVISION

I was able to get an overview of the local authority's daycare provision by initially interviewing senior staff in its three day nurseries. The three officers-in-charge could remember back to 1974–5, when the day nurseries were first opened. Indeed, these three women had worked in those same day nurseries, initially as nursery officers, then as deputies and finally as officers-in-charge for most of that time. Initially all the day nursery places had been full-time, with many offered to children of working parents and particularly to those of working single parents who included 'solicitors' and teachers' children'. These day nurseries had in the early 1970s offered extended day (8 a.m.–6 p.m.) year-round, town-wide provision, and many places were offered to babies.

Daycare becomes linked with child protection

By the late 1970s the allocation of day nursery places had radically changed. The Social Services committee had accepted the DHSS specifications for admissions to day nurseries (circular 37/68), which included meeting the needs of one-parent families. In fact by 1976 nearly all the children attending were not just priority, but were 'highest priority cases'. These cases were where social workers were concerned that children needed protection from possible child abuse. Significantly, although the day nurseries had the potential to offer fifty places, there were vacancies because of the necessity to reduce operational costs. Pressure for 'emergency places' was so great, however, that continuity for the individual child was not a high priority. When a place was offered to a family it was time-limited and it could be withdrawn if more urgent 'cases' needed places. During this period marked by 'child abuse panic' (Fox-Harding 1991) a daycare place was seen, like a one-off 'poverty payment' for food and gas, as preventing the reception of a child into care.

In this way the *dearth* of places, the result both of initial under-funding and on-going cost-cutting, signified the lack of importance placed on daycare as part of strategic planning for children's services. The *sharing* of places and the heavily weighted criteria for allocating places signified the move from daycare 'as a service in its own right' (Cannan 1988) to 'a scarce resource to be allocated by social workers to demoralised parents' (Penn 1984).

By 1976 in this local authority the average age of children attending the day nursery was 3 years and the unit cost per place was around £1,000 per annum, as opposed to approximately £500 for a nursery school place, £375 for a nursery class and £254 for early admission to primary school. While parents using the day nurseries were charged a daily rate (£1 maximum: ability to contribute judged on a standard assessment of income and allowances) the costs to the local authority were high because staff ratios were much higher than for 3-year-olds in the local education authority nursery units. Day nursery staff, who were all NNEB-trained, were by the late 1970s working with a high concentration of children with severe developmental and behavioural problem'. Children were generally offered part-time places between the hours of 9.30 and 3.30; they were often transported in from their homes by Social Services escort drivers.

Pathologising families

Families using these daycare services were immediately pathologised, since having a daycare place implied either neglect or abuse on the part of the parent (Donzelot 1980). It is easy to see how the structural relationship between the 'professional' day workers and the parent as a 'client' could become increasingly unequal. Daycare staff often viewed parents as damaged, 'a view difficult to reconcile with community work principles of the necessity of engaging residential action to improve their own lives' (Cannan 1988). Despite the fact that many of the day nursery staff were younger and much less experienced than the parents of the children in their care, they felt themselves to be, and were seen, as the authoritative professionals with all the knowledge and expertise (Ferri and Saunders 1991). In my study the youngest, least experienced member of the day nursery staff reflected these views:

> We [the staff] can't change anything, they are more influenced by parents than us, blood's thicker than water. They're just dead replicas of their parents; in 20 years' time their children will come into the day nursery. There's no way they'll change.

NEW FORMS OF DAYCARE

In the late 1970s and early 1980s in response to DES and DHSS circulars (March 1976) recommending an integrated approach to setting up services for young children, Social Services and the Education departments in this local authority set up two experimental provisions for under-fives. In this chapter I will refer to only one of these new services, a day nursery set up on traditional lines which was attached to an education nursery unit.

I have described the other centre, a fully integrated education and care provision with a multi-disciplinary staff group elsewhere (Whalley 1993).

The concept of combining daycare and nursery education, under 'separate but complementary management', was not a new idea (Ferri *et al.* 1981). The danger was that here as elsewhere the difference in belief systems, staffing, pay and conditions, and management styles would prevent the two units from ever offering a coherent approach to working with young children of the same age. In the daycare unit parents would have to pay and were offered year-round extended day provision in a service run exclusively by NNEB- trained staff. In the adjacent education nursery unit, teachers and NNEBs offered free, school-day school-term provision. Although the 15-ft outdoor covered play area was shared by the two units, the children from the two establishments rarely used it at the same time. Ironically, when the education nursery unit allowed the children to go out to play it coincided with the daycare unit's indoor rest and quiet time. On one occasion I observed a day nursery child who had been very distressed the previous day kissing his brother good-bye as he left him to attend the education nursery unit. On another occasion a day nursery child playing in the 'shared' outside play space saw his brother playing in the education nursery unit. He asked to go to him and staff from each unit lifted the children so that they could give each other a cuddle – through the window.

THE NEW ROLE OF THE DAY NURSERY IN THE 1980s

The two traditional day nurseries and the new experimental unit seemed to be increasingly marginalised. Although there was a growing recognition in the local authority that 'removing a child from a poor relationship with its mother for ten hours a day five days a week is not necessarily the best way of improving that relationship' (Challis 1981), the day nurseries were still largely seen as a safety net for social workers preoccupied with child protection and family stress. One Social Services line manager commented 'The day nursery was part of a very unclear and vague movement away from looking at Johnny to looking at Johnny and his family.'

Different belief systems

While nursery nurses in the education nursery unit identified their main concerns as child-centred (i.e. promoting children's social and emotional growth, stimulating their educational development and preparing them for entry into the first school), nursery nurses in the day nursery setting emphasised promoting children's social development. The officer-in-charge believed children 'should be offered warmth and comfort, other things are by the by . . . we offer nursery education with home comforts thrown in'. She believed the day nursery should 'never-close', it should always be available to give the children the 'caring, comfortable, stimulating experiences, . . . that *normal* homes would give children that these children aren't getting'. It became clear that day nursery staff's aims and objectives were far-reaching and sometimes appeared idealistic. They ranged from 24-hour-a-day child protection, to a kind of all-embracing Peter Pan-like world of warmth and security which had little to do with any objective reality. Few day nursery staff had ever home-visited the families they worked with, and in reality the maximum number of hours any child spent in the day nursery was around 20 hours per week. Day nursery staff seemed to have a limited awareness of what was happening to the children for the other 148 hours a week.

THE DAY NURSERY CURRICULUM

Chris Athey's (1990) call for a 'more conscious and articulated pedagogy' to help early years workers extend children's thinking with worthwhile curriculum content has not gone unheard in some nurseries (Bruce 1991; Bartholomew and Bruce 1993). In these nurseries staff have greatly increased their understanding as to how children learn, and through close observation and training have increased their understanding of children's thinking and their skills in supporting and extending children's learning. Clearly the National Curriculum and the spectre of base-line assessments has also influenced both nursery teachers and, to a more limited extent, day nursery staff (Sylva 1991).

A laissez-faire approach

From my logged observations in the day nursery setting, however, staff had a fairly laissez-faire approach towards providing an environment in which young children could learn. I was not able to see much planning for children's play and day nursery staff commented 'we take it as it comes'. The officer-in-charge's position was 'to leave it to the girls to do, day by day'. Several of the day nursery staff expressed the view that with their enhanced staff ratios they could offer 'just as much play materials as the nursery class next door', and this was observably true. Perhaps because numbers were very low in the day nursery, considerable amounts of time were spent in laying out materials in an attractive manner and activities were varied from day to day. A great deal of art work had been done, with great care, by the staff in the day nursery and it was displayed around the rooms. The day nursery rooms were divided up like those in the nursery unit into quiet carpeted areas with floor mats, trucks and bricks, a hospital corner, a book corner, and a home corner. Sand, an easel and paint and play dough were also generally available in the day nursery.

There was no reference to any planning for individual children in the day nursery. Very few cognitive goals were mentioned although the word 'stimulation' was used repeatedly. Words like self-confidence and self-esteem were not used, nor was there any reference to providing an environment in which children could make decisions (Bruner 1980; Bronfenbrenner 1979; Watt 1987).

Day nursery staff had strong, rescuing motives and genuine concern with the struggle 'their children' might well experience in breaking free from poverty and 'parental under-stimulation'. They did not perceive other aspects of edu-care to be important, i.e. enabling children to make good choices; enabling children to feel strong; enabling children to question and challenge; and teaching children how to negotiate. The officer-in-charge went so far as to reiterate the previously recorded comments of her youngest member of staff. She said working in the day nursery 'felt like coming home', because she was now working with the children of the children she had worked with over the last 17 years in other daycare establishments run by the same local authority.

DIRECT WORK WITH CHILDREN

'Insecurity in knowledge leads to rigidity in teaching' (DES 1983 in Athey 1990).

Alongside the broad objectives the day nursery staff held around 'a free play' approach it was also possible to observe some 'structured play' and some teaching of basic, (nursery nurse determined) skills. The day nursery staff used a lot of commenting and reflecting language with children which included mainly commanding and directing rather than listening (Tizard and Hughes 1984). The youngest nursery assistant in the day nursery constantly worked with individual children teaching them to say 'Ta' or 'Thank-you'.

CARING FOR CHILDREN

Great attention was paid in the day nursery to the children's separation anxieties, then emotional and physical needs. The children in the day nursery were cuddled and greeted when they arrived and siblings were kept together in family groups.

Some staff in the day nursery did appear to be uncomfortable with withdrawn or distressed children and failed to comfort them. One child who had cried for most of the morning was told to 'stop crying'. He had his jumper taken off without being asked if that was what he wanted, and when he continued to cry and said he was cold he was taken out into the sunshine without consultation and still crying. When he was finally asked if he wanted to go inside he did and played with a car on a table by himself. Several hours later he was still tearful while having his birthday cake in nursery.

Day nursery staff seemed particularly concerned with the need to 'potty-train' children, although most of the children were in the 2–3-year-old bracket and were fairly self-motivated. In practice day nursery staff were as concerned with toileting as they were with teaching the children to say 'Ta'. Indeed in terms of the daily records kept by day nursery staff toileting, eating and manners were seen as very important.

EXTRACTS FROM DAILY RECORDS

M Two wees in potty – quite defiant, and very demanding. Speaks well.
N Came in lovely and had a cuddle. Had a funny at dinner time but when told to he ate it; very tired by dinner time.
S Two thank-yous very clear. Was sent from table when she refused to say it. Beautifully turned out today.
J Lovely, very obliging.

P Aims and goals – colours, touch toes, heel- and toe-walking, ten steps on line, walk on tiptoe, run.
J Used potty three times.
O Very strong-willed.
R Very lethargic and near to tears.
S Seemed better but a bit lost and upset.
D Late.

Strong-willed, determined children in the daycare setting were generally described as disruptive; children who were articulate and confident as 'always wanting to have their own way' (Steedman 1988; Walkerdine 1985).

LINKS WITH PARENTS

My research study was very much concerned with staff attitudes to parents, their beliefs about parents and the role that parents had in the day nursery setting. Since this chapter is primarily concerned with the experiences of the children I will confine myself to a few observations.

Local parents were very clear about the role of the day nursery: 'it only takes desperate cases. My kid's not over active and I'm not beating him up so my case isn't desperate enough.' Another parent commented: 'the day nursery is for problem children, parents have to attend, that's part of their growing up, their education.' One member of the day nursery staff who lived in the local community believed that there was a real stigma attached to attending the day nursery: 'some parents are afraid their relatives will know, some don't care.'

Despite these comments parents did not seem to find it hard to come into the day nursery and drop their children off. The day nursery staff placed a much greater emphasis on flexibility than the nursery education staff. Day nursery parents often stayed for some time, some had a cup of coffee, others felt free to cuddle their children, or to leave them alone. Conversations between staff and parents tended to focus on toileting and feeding. Beyond this 'chatting' was seen as the major interaction with parents and day nursery staff appeared to feel they had successfully engaged the parent (mother) if she had stayed to have a chat for five minutes. I recorded several examples of lost opportunities in these exchanges such as when a parent said, *in desperation*. 'Nat plays me up awful when I get home' and his day nursery officer replied 'He did two lovely wees in his potty'.

CHARACTERISTICS OF THE DAY NURSERY SERVICES

There seemed to be several characteristics common to both the combined daycare and education centre and the two traditional day nurseries where I met senior staff. My extended observations in the new provision also meant I could draw out some key issues:

1 Day nurseries are held back from becoming relevant, accessible and exciting early-years services by their historical association with child abuse and neglect.
2 Because there are enormous demands on the small numbers of available places, the 'deprivation' rather than the 'prevention' model prevails. Day nurseries are seen as a stigmatised resource for problem families rather than as a support for working parents or as an education-care service for local children.
3 The most senior and most experienced staff in day nurseries are obliged to spend most of their time in administrative or domestic duties and are therefore unable to spend time appropriately with children or working alongside colleagues (Richman and McGuire 1988; DES 1988).
4 Staff in the day nursery appeared to be locked into the widely held beliefs of the 1970s and 1980s regarding the need for compensatory education to stimulate children from 'working-class' homes. They did not seem to be aware of more recent research suggesting nursery staff might well have something to learn from parent–child interactions (Tizard and Hughes 1984), and that parents, as their children's first educators, can make a major contribution to work in early years settings (Athey 1990; Bruce 1991).
5 Workers from other disciplines seemed to have very little understanding as to what the day nurseries were really offering.
6 The day nursery curriculum offered very little challenge to young children. In some cases the nursery curriculum could be described as the 'equivalent of lobotomy' (Nancy Elliot, quoted in David 1990).
7 Day nursery staff focused on hugging, holding, helping and directing rather than on negotiation or making informed choices; children were not encouraged to take risks or make decisions.

8   Parents (principally women) were often stereotyped as inadequate, and uncaring, and as wanting to 'dump' their children. Parents were often resented.
9   Day nursery staff were very reluctant to give up their position of power vis-à-vis parents and did not seem clear about why they should develop relationships with parents.

THE WAY FORWARD

Carrying out this research and writing it up has been a powerful experience for me as a practitioner. Watching female colleagues struggling with inappropriate role definitions, dysfunctional management systems and in a poor working environment has not left me feeling comfortable. Staff in day nurseries are often working with parents whose backs are against the wall and with confused and unhappy children. I have sometimes been very uncomfortable with the practice I have observed and I also understand that the day nursery staff genuinely believed in what they were doing.

Day nurseries have an increasingly important role to play in the network of services that parents with young children need and want. Children have a right to the best possible education and care. Staff working within day nurseries need to challenge their own practice, demand greater recognition for what they do, better conditions of service and enhanced training. In that way, they would be able to see themselves as members of a 'proud profession' undertaking one of the most important roles in society.

REFERENCES

Athey, C. (1990) *Extending Thought in Young Children.* London, Paul Chapman Publishing.
Bain, A. and Barnett, L. (1980) *The Design of a Daycare System in Nursery Setting for Children Under 5.* Tavistock, Institute Research Project for DHSS.
Bartholomew, L. and Bruce, T. (1993) *Getting to Know You.* Sevenoaks, Hodder & Stoughton.
Bronfenbrenner, U. (1979) *The Ecology of Human Development.* Cambridge, MA, Harvard University Press.
Bruce, T. (1991) *Time to Play.* Sevenoaks, Hodder & Stoughton.
Bruner, J. (1980) *Under 5 in Britain.* London, Grant McIntyre.
Cannan, C. (1986) 'Sanctuary or Stigma?', *Community Care*, 22 May, 612, 14–17.
—— (1988) 'Images of domesticity. the work of the family centre', in *Block*

3 *Private Troubles and Public Issues*. Milton Keynes, Open University Press Social Science.

Challis, L. (1981) *Confusion and Conspiracy in Childcare and the State*. London, Research Papers published by National Childcare Campaign.

Clarke-Stewart, A. (1989) 'Infant daycare: maligned or malignant?', *American Psychologist*, 44, 266–73.

Condry, G. (1986) 'Co-ordination, co-operation and control in pre-school services', D.Phil (unpub.) Department of Sociology, University of Surrey.

David, T. (1990) *Under 5 – Under Educated?*. Milton Keynes, Open University Press.

DES (1988) *Combined Provision for the Under Fives: The Contribution of Education*. HMI DS4J.

—— (1990) *Starting with Quality: Report of the Committee of Inquiry into the Quality of the Educational Experience Offered to 3- and 4-year-olds*. London, HMSO.

Donzelot, J. (1980) *The Policity of Families Welfare Versus the State*. London, Hutchinson.

Ferri, E., Birchall, D., Gingell, V. and Gipps, C. (1981) *Combined Nursery Centres*. London, NCB/Macmillan.

Ferri, E. and Saunders, A. (1991) *Parents, Professionals and Pre-school Centres. A Study of Barnardo's Provision*. London, NCB.

Fletcher, C. (1991) 'An analysis of practitioner research', in B. Broad and C. Fletcher (eds) *Practitioner Research into Social Work: From Experiences to an Agenda*. Cranfield , Cranfield Institute of Technology.

Fox-Harding, L. (1991) *Perspectives in Childcare Policy*. London, Longman.

Garland, C. and White, S. (1980) *Children and Day Nurseries*. London, Grant McIntyre.

Hennessy, E., Martin, S., Moss, P. and Melhuish, E. (1992) *Children and Daycare: Lessons from Research*. London, Paul Chapman.

Marshall, T. (1982) 'Infant care: a day nursery under the microscope', *Social Work Service*, 32.

Melhuish, E. and Moss, P. (1991) *Daycare for Young Children: International Perspectives*. London, Routledge.

Moss, R. and Melhuish, E. (eds) (1991) *Current Issues in Daycare for Young Children*. London, HMSO.

Northamptonshire County Council (1976) *Provision for the Under 5's in Northamptonshire*. Northampton, NCC.

Penn, H. (1984) *Nursery Education What Future?*. London, Local Government Campaign Unit.

Reason, P. and Marshall, J. (1986) 'Research as Personal Process', in D. Bould and V. Griffin (eds) *Understanding Adult Learning: From the Learner's Perspective*.

Richman, N. and McGuire, J. (1988) 'Institutional characteristics and staff behaviour in day nurseries', *Children and Society*, 2.2, 138–51.

Riley, D. (1983) *Work in the Nursery*. London, Virago Press.

Schweinhart, L.J. and Weikart, D. (1980) *Young Children Growing Up: The Effects of the Perry Pre-school Programme on Youths through Age 15*. Yipsilanti, MI, The High Scope Education Research Foundation.

Steedman, C. (1988) 'The mother made conscious', in M. Woodhead and

A. McGrath (eds) *Family School and Society*. Milton Keynes, The Open University.

Sylva, K. (1991) in P. Moss and E. Melhuish *Current Issues in Day Care for Young Children*. London, HMSO.

Tizard, B. and Hughes, M. (1984) *Young Children Learning*. London, Fontana.

Van der Eyken, W. (1984) *Day Nurseries in Action: A National Study of Local Authority Day Nurseries in England (1975–1983)*. Report to the Department of Health, Bristol University, Department of Child Health Research Unit.

Walkerdine, V. (1985) 'Child development and gender: the making of teachers and learners in nursery classrooms in early childhood education', in C. Adelman (ed.) *History Policy and Practice*. Reading, Bulmershe.

Watt, J.S. (1977) *Co-operation in Pre-school Education*. London, SSRC.

—— (1987) 'Continuity in early education', in M.M. Clark (ed.) 'Roles, responsibilities and relationships in the education of the young child', Birmingham University, *Education Review*, 13.

Webb, J.M. (1991) 'Forgotten years', *Early Years*, 12, 1, Autumn, 8–13.

Whalley, M. (1982) 'A description and analysis of the development and organisation of education and daycare for under 5's from a community education perspective', MA (unpub.), Leicester University.

—— (1993) *Learning to be Strong: Setting Up a Neighbourhood Service for Under 5's and Families*. Sevenoaks, Hodder & Stoughton.

Chapter 13

Training to work with young children

Audrey Curtis

Government policy for more than a decade has been to encourage a diversity of daycare provision for children under mandatory school age.

One result of this policy is that the pattern of childcare services in the UK is both complex and confusing. There exists a large number of statutory, voluntary and private agencies, ranging from home care with a registered childminder to attendance at a primary school in a Year I classroom. In spite of this variety there is a severe shortage of high quality daycare services available to parents in a system which lacks integration and coordination of care and education for young children.

High quality provision is closely linked to the training of early years workers. At present, because the services for young children are administratively divided across three government departments, education, health and care, 'the child is divided into bits to be educated, bits to be vaccinated and bits to be cared for', as Denise Hevey so aptly put it in a recent lecture (1992). This artificial division is perpetuated in the training courses for early years workers.

At present each of the agencies concerned with young children and their families has its own training programmes leading to different types of qualifications and there is little opportunity for progression or professional development. The Rumbold Committee (DES 1990) called for a determined effort to be made 'to bring greater clarity and coherence across the field of courses and qualifications for workers with the under fives'.

Not only is there a lack of coherence and progression, but many concerned with the training of early childhood educators query the appropriateness of some of the existing qualifications to meet the needs of those working with young children.

These discussions have been on-going for some time, but recent legislation in education, care and health has made it essential that the issues are addressed with some urgency.

The Education Reform Act (DES 1988) is having a considerable impact upon even the youngest children in the school system and indirectly upon the curriculum of the private and voluntary sectors in the nursery years (Sylva *et al.* 1992). It is not just the pressures from the National Curriculum which are affecting the children under statutory school age, but as more and more schools opt out of local authority control and the power of the local authorities weakens, we see the disappearance of more and more early-years inspectors and advisers. The new inspection teams may not include a person with expertise in the field of early child- hood and as a result there will be no one to monitor the quality of nursery classes and schools or to protest when governors replace a nursery teacher with someone who is less appropriately trained. Furthermore the new inspection guidelines do not appear to be appropriate for evaluating early-years programmes, although I understand that there are to be new ones issued in the near future which will take into account the special nature of early years education.

Modifications in the management and funding of the National Health Service, with its changes in relationship between clients and providers, are likely to affect the child community services.

However, the most important change relates to the implementation of the Children Act 1989, in the autumn of 1991, as this has far-reaching implications for the local authorities who have statutory requirements regarding children in need and new responsibilities with regard to registration.

The concept of need is widely defined to include 'those whose health and development is unlikely to be achieved or maintained or may be significantly impaired without the proper provision of services'. Local authorities are also empowered to make provision for children not in need, although the Guidance (DoH 1991) makes it clear that public funds are unlikely to be sufficient to provide for all parents who require services.

Under the Children Act 1989 local authorities are forced to look closely at the need to coordinate services for children under 8 as they are now legally required to:

(a) provide daycare services for young children in need;
(b) review all services for children under 8 every three years; and
(c) register and inspect services.

David (1992) identified more than thirty-six groups of workers who could be required to cooperate in the best interests of young children, ranging from lawyers, doctors and social workers to teachers, voluntary workers and students. This extent of inter-agency cooperation, if it is to succeed, along with the two other major pieces of recent legislation, must have far-reaching implications for the training of early childhood workers, whose role is to both care for *and* educate young children.

In this chapter I intend to discuss some of the issues arising from these changes and consider the proposals that are being made to offer early childhood educators an appropriate preparation for working collaboratively with young children and their families.

WHO ARE THE EDUCATORS OF YOUNG CHILDREN?

I shall be adopting the same procedure as the Rumbold Committee and using the term educator to cover the wide range of people who work with young children and their families, unless the meaning is more specific. Who are the main educators involved with young children and their families and how are they trained? As Hevey (1992) pointed out, the vast majority of people working with young children are both unqualified and underpaid. Most, predominantly women, are working either as childminders or in the voluntary sector with little or no training. Many attend short non-award-bearing courses, which often receive little recognition from the local authorities. The many women in the playgroup movement, who are responsible for thousands of children each day, are frequently minimally qualified and their qualifications are not necessarily recognised within the community.

The majority of trained professionals in the area of childcare and education are nursery officers who may be employed in a variety of sectors; education, health, social services and the independent sector. Their two-year training will have given them a basic understanding of the needs of children aged 0–8 years, but many believe that the initial course is not rigorous enough, although the new modular diploma in Nursery Nursing and the B Tech qualification in Nursery Nursing are of a higher academic standard.

The two groups of professionals with the longest training are the teachers and the social workers. In both cases their training may have been generic. For the social worker this probably means that they will have little or no knowledge of child development and for some teachers, even though they have specialised in the early years (3–9 years), the requirements of the Council for the Accreditation of Teacher Education (CATE) will have prevented them from spending substantial periods of time working with and studying about children aged 3–5 years. Whatever course they followed it is unlikely that they will have much knowledge of children from birth to 3 years.

Social workers are almost always employed by the local Social Service departments, while teachers are chiefly to be found in the education sector. In recent years, there has been a move by some local authorities to adopt the philosophy of 'educare' and place all the care and education of children from birth upwards under the auspices of the Education Department, rather than the usual pattern of devolving responsibility for the under-threes to the local Social Service departments and the over-threes to education. As a result teachers have been recruited to some local authority day nurseries and family centres as the person in charge. Moves of this kind are to be welcomed, although I understand that in the current economic climate these innovations are at risk.

IS THE CURRENT TRAINING FOR EARLY YEARS EDUCATORS ADEQUATE?

For the large numbers of workers who have not had an opportunity for training, the obvious answer must be an unqualified 'No'. The introduction of National Vocational Qualifications (NVQs) in Child Care and Education in February 1992 might eventually offer to many the opportunity to demonstrate that they are both competent and have the underpinning knowledge and understanding to perform 'roles to the standards expected in employment'.

But are the professionals who are expected to implement the new regulations adequately prepared? Under the present training policy it is probably not feasible for social workers to spend more time on child development and the understanding of the educational needs of young children, although it is clearly desirable that they have this knowledge if they are to be responsible for the registering and monitoring of daycare services.

Likewise can teacher training, which is currently focusing more and more upon the needs of the subject disciplines of the National

Curriculum, properly prepare teachers to work efficiently with young children and their families?

In recent years the emphasis upon psychology and child development long associated with the training of early-years teachers has given way to the subject disciplines. Courses must now have at least 50 per cent of their time devoted to National Curriculum subjects and even greater changes are currently under review.

When CATE introduced its requirements in 1985, early childhood educators in the institutes of higher education argued loud and long for the inclusion of child development and/or psychology as a subject discipline for the B.Ed. courses. No one wanted teachers of the younger age-range children to be considered less academically qualified than those working with older children, but it was felt that these disciplines could be as rigorous as any of the subjects in the National Curriculum.

However, the argument was lost. If the trainee teachers are to obtain qualified teacher status they must meet the approved criteria and this means an increase in the number of hours spent on the subjects of the National Curriculum with a proportionate decrease in the amount of time spent on the study of child development and allied subjects. Those of us working as early-childhood educators in the institutes of higher education were and are faced with a real dilemma. If we try to amend the early-years teaching course, so that teachers are trained to ensure that children and their families receive the highest 'educare' possible, will we be guilty of undermining the profession and producing nursery teachers who are regarded as 'second-class citizens'? On the other hand, if we accept the current situation we may not be preparing teachers adequately to meet the needs of young children and their families in the twenty-first century.

A dilemma which has been heightened by the latest government proposals to be considered by CATE (March 1993), which could result in non-graduate status for teachers in the nursery and infant schools. Quality care and education of young children requires teachers to have as high a level of skills and competences and knowledge as teachers of older children and any attempt to degrade their status or professionalism must be resisted at all costs.

A close look at existing patterns of training for those working with under-fives raises two important issues. First, no one course appears to offer the knowledge, skills and competences required in a multi-disciplinary approach to provision for young children and their families. Secondly, the majority of the current non-graduate-training programmes are discrete and do not offer opportunities for progression in their qualifications.

WHAT SORT OF TRAINING FOR THE FUTURE?

Before attempting to answer this question, consideration must be given to the basic skills and competences that all educators need if they are to function effectively.

Work with young children and their families requires an ability to:

1   display an awareness and sensitivity to the needs of others;
2   communicate by all possible means with colleagues, parents, other agencies and above all with children;
3   have a sound knowledge of child development and how children learn;
4   have a knowledge of the laws relating to families;
5   plan programmes which ensure both continuity and progression;
6   observe and evaluate children's progress; and
7   respect children and their individual cultural, social and personal differences.

For those who are in leadership roles they need also the ability to understand the views of others in order to carry out their management duties effectively; to be able to encourage the personal development of team members. A comprehensive list of the qualities required by early childhood educators can be found in Curtis (1992).

For more than a decade disquiet has existed among groups of people concerned with the training of early childhood personnel and they have been meeting to discuss how we might produce a high-quality training in 'educare'. We believed that social workers, teachers and others involved with the care and education of young children should spend at least part of their training in joint seminars so that each would have some understanding of the issues raised in the different professions. Our discussion foundered, most probably because the climate was not ready for a major change not only in training, but in attitudes towards cooperation and coordination of services.

However, new legislation and the economic climate, along with an increased awareness of the need to provide better career opportunities for the many thousands of women working in the field of early childhood, encouraged a group of people to meet yet again to look into these issues.

In 1991 the Early Years Unit at the National Children's Bureau convened a group of early years trainers and advisers to discuss the issue of the future training needs for under-fives workers. The idea originated from a challenging paper by Pam Calder and although, as was to be expected, there were differences of opinion between the group there was general consensus concerning

the need for a new graduate level 'educare' qualification, which can either provide a route into teaching or social work, or provide an adequate preparation for working in early childhood settings in its own right.

(Pugh 1992)

Several universities have, or are in the process of, taking up the challenge and promoting a degree in early-childhood studies. Most of the degrees are modular, and all have a multi-disciplinary approach allowing students to select the modules most suited to their needs. Naturally there are differences in emphasis, but all courses are marked by a strong child development component covering the age range 0–8 years and the underpinning knowledge of how children think and learn. Other modules will include social policy, management strategies, counselling and working with parents and other adults in a multi-disciplinary setting. It is envisaged that such degrees will give students the appropriate theoretical framework and underpinning knowledge to work with young children and their families. However, they will still require relevant postgraduate qualifications if they wish to go into teaching or social work.

Through careful planning and organisation it may well be possible for graduates from these courses to acquire qualified teacher status or social work recognition. Although entry to these courses is normally by the standard A level or equivalent route, there are also opportunities for experienced workers to present evidence of prior learning in place of the traditional entry qualifications. In at least one of the courses accredited prior learning (APL) may lead to candidates being given credits towards their degree. For the first time it appears that previous experience is being accepted as making a valuable contribution to early years training at university level.

ACCREDITATION OF COURSES

At present the question of accreditation is a complex one. Teaching and social work qualifications are accredited by two separate bodies, CATE and CCETSW, but many feel that there should be a single agency to accredit all early years training. Such a body would look at not only early years degrees and existing teacher training and social work courses, but also at the many non-graduate qualifications currently in existence. These include the diplomas in Nursery Nursing awarded by the Nursery Nurse Examination Board and the Business and Technical Council, and the shorter programmes leading to qualifications granted by City and Guilds, the Preschool Playgroups Association and National Childminding Association, etc.

A single body would be able to monitor levels of study both within and between awards and look at the overlap with qualifications in other areas like hospital play work, residential care and children with special needs, etc. As we move more and more into distance learning and the accreditation of prior learning it becomes increasingly important that there is an agency which has a clear overview of the field of early education and care.

NATIONAL OCCUPATIONAL STANDARDS

The introduction of the National Vocational Qualifications in Child Care and Education at Levels 2 and 3 in February 1992 should help to ensure quality assurance in this field. These new National Occupational Standards will assist in bridging the gap between care and education, since they require candidates to demonstrate competence in the work place by performing their roles to the 'standards expected in employment'. There is a substantial common core of units at each of the existing levels and an additional two to four units which form separate endorsements allowing for a degree of specialisation, i.e. work with babies, or group care and education.

The NVQs in Child Care and Education, like those in other fields, have been designed to allow for progression. Some units are part of the core at both levels 2 and 3, while others are extended at the higher level. In some instances level-2 units are replaced by more complex functions at the next level. At present these are the only two levels in existence but it is hoped that eventually candidates will be able to progress to levels 4 and 5. When and *if* this comes about, we shall have professionals trained in a multi-disciplinary approach to work with young children and their families.

Careful inspection of the NVQs shows that the standards have been devised to take into account the two basic principles of the Children Act 1989, i.e. that the interests of the children are paramount and that all aspects of services and provision should operate in conjunction with parents.

The act also takes into consideration the need to promote anti-discriminatory practice, the need to take into account the ethnic and cultural background of the children and the importance of integrating children with special needs into mainstream settings wherever possible. The occupational standards for work with young children and their families have incorporated these principles into their units and an important part of assessor training by the awarding bodies – Council for Early Years Awards (CEYA) and the Joint Awarding Body (JABs) – is to ensure that these principles are part of the daily good practice carried out by candidates in their early childhood work place settings.

These standards of good practice were developed in cooperation with several thousand practitioners and managers throughout the country and should ultimately lead to greatly improved standards in the field of childcare and education.

Besides having the potential to improve practice, these NVQs will offer mature, experienced, hitherto unqualified workers with opportunities to gain recognised qualifications. These qualifications will also be recognised by the more traditional awarding bodies like universities for entry into higher-level courses.

Critics of these new qualifications have argued that it will be impossible to set national standards across the different work-place settings. As an external verifier for CEYA I am well aware of this problem, but believe that there are sufficient controls in place to ensure quality assurance. It is in the best interests of all those concerned with these new national vocational standards to ensure that quality is maintained.

Ultimately it is hoped that NVQs will become a requirement in the childcare and education field. Providing training and assessment is not too expensive, it should become a requisite for all working in early childhood settings, both institutional and in the home to obtain an NVQ. At present many local authorities and the national associations are encouraging their workers to come forward to register for these qualifications and in some instances are providing financial support to workers.

CONCLUSION

Early childhood care and education in the UK is currently at a crossroads. The Children Act 1989 has forced us to recognise two important factors. First, that it is imperative for agencies to cooperate in the best interests of children and their families and second, that none of the existing professional courses offer appropriate training for this work.

The introduction of NVQs at levels 2 and 3 should ultimately provide appropriate quality at the non-graduate level, but since it is unlikely that the higher levels will be introduced in the foreseeable future it is to the early childhood studies and B.Ed. degree courses that we need to look.

In pressing for a multi-disciplinary early years teacher education course which meets the needs of young children and their families, we may find ourselves arguing for a qualification which is seen as different from other primary teachers. If this were to happen there is a danger that early years specialists could be seen by sceptics as 'second class' and they would not have the opportunity of working with older age-range children as happens today. We should then be guilty of limiting the career progression of many early years teachers who in the future may wish to become head teachers of primary schools and whose experience with young children would be invaluable.

Furthermore, we could be placing early years teachers in a situation where they would be like their counterparts in Germany and Denmark, where both pay and status is inferior to that of primary school teachers.

The challenge for advocates of quality early childhood education is to find ways of ensuring that entrants into the profession have an appropriate training which allows them to cater for the best interests of young children and that their professionalism is recognised in terms of salary and conditions of service.

REFERENCES

Calder, P. (1990) 'The training of nursery workers: the need for a new approach', *Children and Society*, 4, 3, 251–60.

Care Sector Consortium (1991) *National Occupational Standards for Working with Young Children and their Families*. London, NCB.

Curtis, A. (1992) 'Training to work in the early years', in G. Pugh (ed.) *Contemporary Issues in the Early Years*. London, Paul Chapman.

David, T. (1992) *The Children Act*. London, OMEP Publication.

DES (1988) *Education Reform Act*. London, HMSO.

—— (1990) *Starting with Quality*, The Rumbold Report. London, HMSO.

DoH (1989) *The Children Act*. London, HMSO.

—— (1991) *The Children Act 1989. Guidance and Regulations*. London, HMSO.

Hevey, D. (1991) 'Final report of the working with under sevens project', Paper presented to the Care Sector Consortium, London, September 1991.

—— (1992) *NVQs and the Future of Early Years Qualifications*. Unpublished paper.

Pugh, G. (1992) *The Future of Training in the Early Years*. London, NCB.

Sylva, K., Blatchford, I. and Johnson, S.(1992) 'The impact of the National Curriculum pre-school practice', *International Journal of Early Childhood*, 24, 1, 41–51.

Chapter 14

Coordinating provision – the story so far in one local authority

Ann Sharp

This chapter is an account of the developments in one local authority, which for over a decade systematically set out to coordinate its under-five provision, and at the same time develop cooperative working with the voluntary sector and the Health Authority. It must be noted, however, that the perspective is that of the author who works in the Education Service and was a central participant in the developments outlined. It must also be said that while this is an account of what happened, any personal views expressed do not necessarily reflect those of the local authority.

BACKGROUND

It is worth a brief reminder of the context in which local authorities made their initial decisions on coordinating services. Following the 1972 White Paper 'Education a Framework for Expansion' and the Department of Education and Science Circular 2/73, local authorities were urged to take into account other services for under-fives when planning the expansion of education, and indeed to 'consider carefully' (para. 17 of the Circular) the role of playgroups when preparing to develop nursery education.

Two significant joint reports were published by the Department of Health and Social Security and the Department of Education and Science: in 1976 on 'Low Cost Day Provision for the Under Fives' and in 1977 on 'Combined Nursery Schools and Day Centres'. At the same time the DHSS and DES jointly issued two circular letters, the first in March 1976 on the Coordination of Local Authority Services for Children Under Five, and the second in January 1978 on the Coordination of Services for All Children Under Five. The second had a much wider perspective and included the voluntary and health sectors as well as Education and Social Service departments.

Nursery education had begun to expand in the 1970s and early admission to reception classes was introduced following Circular 2/73. By 1980 a number of joint centres had opened in England. Sheffield followed this pattern, expanding nursery classes establishing early admission classes and in 1980 three new types of under-fives provision were opened which had been jointly planned and set up by the Social Services and Education departments. At the same time it had established an Advisory Committee for Under Fives, on which were represented all the groups working with under-fives. This type of coordinating committee had been established by approximately half of the local authorities in England and Wales by 1980.

For many years prior to 1980, joint committees had been established in Sheffield to coordinate Special Needs, and provision was used effectively by both departments, the voluntary sector and the health service. This formed a useful basis on which early developments could move forward, and these links have been maintained and developed over the years.

FRAMEWORK

The authority began the decade therefore, with a commitment in two council departments of working towards a coordinated service. It had councillors, officers and advisers in Social Services and Education who were working together within a clear framework. The subsequent developments were principally based on four premises incorporated into the anti-racist and anti-sexist policies of the Council.

'Educare'

Premise – that the division between 'care' and 'education' should be removed. 'The aims for under-fives are basically the same as those for any other phase with the exception that very young children need a considerable amount of care. Care and education for the under-fives are complementary and inseparable' (Education, Science, Arts Committee Report 1988). Later the Rumbold Report (DES 1990) used the term Educator to describe all those who work with young children. The two Sheffield departments saw each group of staff as having knowledge and expertise to contribute to the other, and jointly providing the best quality 'educare' for young children.

Coherence

Premise – that some logical cohesion should bring together under-fives provision. 'One of the strengths and weaknesses of our provision for children under statutory school age is its diversity. There are few countries where parents have so much choice, although the different kinds of provision is uneven' (Curtis 1992). The departments wanted to try to make more efficient use of resources and present them to parents in a corporate fashion, so that parents could make informed decisions about where to send their children. This meant setting up methods of working more closely with the Voluntary Sector and the Health Authority in collecting and distributing information, and placing children.

Flexibility

Premise – that a flexible service should be provided to meet the needs of young children and their families. In particular, attention should be paid to the length of time that a service was provided. The 1980 Education Act enabled provision in nursery schools and classes to be made on a flexible basis rather than on set times, and so provided an opportunity for rethinking the hours provided.

Quality

Premise – that provision should be of 'good quality'. This has been an extremely important aspect. Councillor Barton, chair of the Education Committee, giving evidence to ESAC in 1988, said 'We believe the quality we have in Sheffield is excellent and we believe we ought to be able to offer high quality provision to all children within the city'. However, because under-five provision is linked to opportunities available (principally for women), both in employment and in training, there have been difficulties in meeting the needs of adults as against the provision for the children of a quality curriculum in whatever setting.

WORKING TOGETHER

Joint centres

As already stated, in 1980 three new schemes jointly planned and run were started in Sheffield. All were open all year 8.00 a.m.–6.00 p.m., two provided places for children under five and one was principally for family support. One was a purpose-built family centre with 40 full-time equivalent (fte) places for under-fives staffed by nursery officers and teachers; the second a day nursery unit with 10 fte places with a nursery class in a nursery first school and the third was a family and community resource centre attached to a nursery school.

There were also plans to open two more family centres for children under 5. Within six months of opening the first centre, the departments reconsidered their plans in the light of operational difficulties which have been well documented in a national framework, such as different terms and conditions of service and different approaches. The problems immediately provided a focus to rethink policy. A new approach was developed to look more closely at neighbourhood schemes and focused on the school structure because it is a universal service for children from 5 years old. The result was Mosborough Townships Under Fives Service, which opened in 1984 and was to provide the model for all the schemes that were planned in Sheffield for the next few years.

The now well-established service provides for 78 fte places with over 100 children accommodated within flexible hours. It is based on two school sites and open all year 8.00 a.m.–6.00 p.m. The 3- and 4-year-olds are accommodated in nursery classes and provision for under-threes is made through a 25 fte-place daycarer scheme. It is managed by three coordinators, two teachers and one social worker with all staff, except the social worker, on the same terms and conditions of service, that is Education. Its organisation has been outlined by Gillian Pugh in *Services for Under Fives – Developing a Co-ordinated Approach* (1988).

The scheme has operated successfully since it began and formal evaluations have been carried out by the Authority. The advent of the Education Reform Act in 1988 has, however, caused problems with the structure. The delegation of budgets to schools means that the local authority no longer has control over the resources. Although this scheme with the cooperation of the governing bodies of the two schools, continues to run as a successful joint venture, ERA has meant that this type of development is having to be rethought.

Project groups

The expansion of the under-fives service across the city was seen as a joint activity and in the early 1980s Education and Social Services set up joint project groups to look at all under-five schemes proposed in the city. In addition to the City Council departments they had representation from local communities, the Preschool Playgroups Association and the Health Authority. Consultation across all user groups was undertaken and a number of projects established. Two new neighbourhood centres opened and eight nursery classes, the design of the latter allowing for any future use for extended hours.

Admission

By 1986 a joint admissions policy for nursery schools and classes, day nurseries and joint centres which incorporated the LEA's policy on 'Rising Five' admission, was agreed by Education and Social Services. It gives a coherent and consistent policy across the local authority which is understood by health visitors, social workers, day nurseries and schools. Crucial in the implementation of this policy are two under-five area coordinator posts which enable the authority to respond in a flexible way to requests which do not match the joint policy. The latest development is the drawing up of a joint application form for admission to nursery schools and classes and day nurseries.

Nursery schools and classes responding to the 1980 Act had begun to provide places which were not of the traditional type; for example, children might start at 3 with two or three half days or two whole days a week. This has met the needs of both the children and families in many areas. Area admission panels were set up to try to make the best use of limited resources. They meet termly and include representation from all those concerned with under-fives: schools, day nurseries, health visitors.

Curriculum

Work with day nurseries on curriculum development started in

1981 and in 1983 was made a part of the new area coordinator posts. On the introduction of the National Curriculum head-teachers of nursery schools and principals of day nurseries established a joint group which now meets regularly. The schools and day nurseries are 'twinned' to ensure that each supports and informs the other of developments. All National Curriculum materials have been distributed to the day nurseries and Social Services staff, together with appropriate SEAC and DES/DFE communications.

The introduction of GEST Activity 11 (DES funding for Under Fives In Service) in 1991–3 gave the opportunity to employ a nursery headteacher full-time to work on curriculum develop-ment in the day nurseries, with childminders and in the voluntary sector.

In-service

In-service courses was an area where it quickly became apparent that work could be done jointly. In 1981 all relevant courses organised by the Education Advisory Service were opened to day nurseries, playgroups, and health visitors. From 1983 courses were added which were specifically designed for inter-disciplinary audiences. These were mainly in the evenings and twilights times and among the topics covered were Structuring Play, Com-munication Skills, Becoming a Writer, Developing a Curriculum and Working with Parents.

Quality assurance

The emphasis on quality provision led during the early 1980s to the drawing up of guidelines for all aspects of under-fives provision. Guidelines for under-five groups in secondary schools, and for creches in the Adult Education Service were drawn up jointly by Education, Social Services and the Health Authority. Social Services produced guidelines for its own provision in day nurseries and the Education Department produced guidance for nursery schools and classes, and for rising five classes. The latter have been updated in 1992 in the light of the Education Reform Act 1988 and the Children Act 1989 (Sheffield LEA 1986, 1987).

The most exciting venture, however, was convening a group representative of all those who work with under-fives, to produce detailed guidelines for registration, inspection and review under the Children Act (DoH 1991). The group was chaired jointly by Education and Social Services and in fifteen months produced 'Quality Criteria for Registration, Inspection and Review in Day care and Education for the Under Fives' (Sheffield LEA 1991).

A need was also identified for a common record across the city for all under-fives and once again a joint group produced a pack on 'Record Keeping for Children Under Five in all Settings' (Sheffield LEA 1991). It is hoped that it will ensure continuity and help to make children's transitions easier.

The Record Pack and the Quality Criteria were distributed to all playgroups, and childminding groups as well as all Education and Social Service establishments. In-service support was given on the ways the pack could be used.

In response to parental requests for help with their children the coordinators produced a pack of activities to do with under-fives called 'Fun Together' which has been used extensively since its publication in 1988.

There has been joint reviewing and monitoring of provision. Following the setting up of Tertiary Colleges, Social Services, Health and Education reviewed the provision and reported to Committee. Education and Social Services have worked together monitoring playgroup quality both at initial registration and subsequently on a regular basis.

NETWORKS

It became very clear by 1981 that coordinating services is more than just creating new schemes: working together involved a radical rethink on everyone's part, and created a need for additional posts to facilitate this. Within the Social Service and Education departments there were already officers and advisers working closely together, but the expansion of work needed more people and in 1983 an under-five area coordinator post funded by the Education Department was created as a pilot project. From that initial project two posts were created on a permanent basis. A multicultural under-fives coordinator post was also established in 1985 in the Education Department with a brief to work within schools and the community and to link with Social Services and the voluntary sector.

Liaison groups

In 1984 the area coordinators began to establish under-five liaison groups across the city. These were based on the work done by the Schools Council on creating networks which would link together and therefore improve children's experiences (Liaison Groups in Early Education 1982). Twenty-two groups were set up within two years and have now become firmly established providing a good city network. Each group has people who work with under-fives in all kinds of settings and includes:

- Bilingual home tutors
- Childcare assistants
- Childminders/daycarers
- Combined centre staff
- Community teachers
- Creche workers
- Day nursery staff
- Dental health nurses
- Ethnic minority child care assistants
- Health visitors and link workers
- Home teachers
- Librarians
- Nursery nurses/officers
- Parent and toddler group staff
- Parents
- Playgroup workers
- PPA representatives
- Schools governors
- Student health visitors
- Student social workers
- Teachers – nursery, infant, first, junior, middle, secondary, special
- Toy library staff
- Women's forum members

The groups meet twice a term and their principal aim is to bring together workers to ensure continuity in transition and support for families but they are also mutual support groups, they ensure that people in an area know each other and are able to work together. They act as joint in-service forums and some of the topics covered by groups are:

- Activities for young children
- Adoption and fostering
- Behaviour clinic
- Behaviour problems
- Black and mixed race children
- Child abuse – child protection
- Children Act 1989
- Children with special needs
- Children's helpline
- Community doctor
- Computers and young children
- Continuity of the curriculum
- Dental health project
- Early literacy development
- Emergent writing
- Healthy teeth
- Homestart
- Hyperactive children
- 'It's Their Future'
- Multicultural education
- Multicultural resources
- Outdoor resources
- Record keeping
- Transition

INFORMATION

Information for parents is essential if they are to make informed choices. Although there was (and still is) a city-wide information brochure, parents have requested more detailed local information. The coordinators have produced detailed booklets for each local area matching the liaison groups and listing all the provision available for under-fives such as nurseries, playgroups, parent and toddler groups, and toy libraries. The booklets are regularly updated and approximately 1,000 copies are distributed free within a local area.

Area coordinator role

In addition to the above the under-five area coordinator posts include the following activities.

Working with Social Services on joint project groups; attending meetings on under-fives funds, toy libraries and support services; meeting regularly with under-fives social workers; attending joint day nursery and education admissions panels; working in day nurseries where requested to give a curriculum input, alongside staff and running in-service groups; contributing to childminding courses.

Working within the Voluntary Sector with Home Start, NSPCC, and the Pre School Playgroups Association, assisting on courses, linking playgroups to schools, meeting regularly with area organisers and leaders.

Working with the Health Sector on training courses and meeting health visitors on a regular basis.

The coordinators visit and collect information, annually, of all under-five numbers and organisations (both nursery and rising five) and on parental activities in all schools. This information enables support to be given as needed. They help set up and subsequently support parent and toddler groups, toy libraries and parent libraries. They help set up and then monitor and advise playgroups on education premises and attend their management meetings. They have set up under-five groups in comprehensive schools, supported them and contributed to the childcare courses for GCSE.

They home visit where parents make special requests regarding admission for under-fives or have some difficulty that needs resolving. They organise and attend area admission panels to coordinate provision on an area basis.

With the introduction of the Children Act these posts were redesignated to 'Early Childhood Education' instead of just under-fives and the work in relation to under-eights and registration of groups on education premises has been given to them.

ORGANISATION

As indicated earlier Sheffield had by 1980 established an Under Fives Advisory Committee. It met on a termly basis and provided a forum for discussion and a venue in which issues could be publicly debated. Out of this committee a joint officer/member working party was established in 1984 to look at daytime childcare in Sheffield. In 1986 the report of the group, 'It's Their Future', was published, setting out the local authority's commitment to a unified service which should be managed by one department only, i.e. Education. An Under Fives Sub-committee of the Education Committee was established in 1987. Plans were drawn up for the redistribution of resources based on nursery classes, to establish a comprehensive unified service across the city which was essentially area-based ('pram pushing' distance). Working groups were set up, existing resources looked at and a plan drawn up for a unified service based on nursery classes and with neighbour-hood support for families.

Early in the development work the consultation papers which resulted in the Education Reform Act of 1988 and the Children Act of 1989 appeared, and presented hurdles to the concept of setting up an under-fives service as set out in 'It's Their Future'. A rethink was needed to take account of the new legislation and once again the departments responded in a positive way. A new strategy was set out in a report, 'Corporate Childcare Strategy – Options for change'. The emphasis is still on having one department to manage the service but the age-range has been extended to 8 following the Children Act and includes Recreation Department as well as Education and Social Services. The Under Fives Committee has become the Young Persons Sub-committee. The provision of places in partnership with employers is being pursued through the 'Child Care through Partnership' project.

WHERE ARE WE NOW?

Difficulties of finance and legislation have meant that all services have not yet been transferred into one department creating a Young Children's service. Gillian Pugh (1992) sets out the problem clearly: 'The Children Act, The Education Reform Act, and indeed the NHS and Community Care Act – all have a clear focus on monitoring, regulating and reviewing services, on quality control and on making information available to consumers/parents. The legislation fails to provide a lead in creating a co-ordinated framework for the development of services and the resources to take that development forward.' The Education (Schools) Act 1992 and the White Paper, 'Framework for Expansion', have also produced difficulties for resourcing services.

There is a clear commitment within Sheffield to the establishment of a Young Children's service and the achievements of the 1980s mean that there is a good basis on which to do this. Indeed, to have a positive cooperative network in the field is a solid foundation on which to create an effective unified service for young children and their families.

The authority was well placed to implement the Children Act because of the established practice of all departments working together, and has set up joint committees within the City Council and with the Health Service to do so.

Finally the first Triennial Review of the Children Act in Sheffield has set out the local authority's positive commitment to a Young Children's Service to ensure that 'care' and 'education' are combined, and that there is coherence, flexibility and quality for all young children.

REFERENCES

Bate, M., Hargreaves, M. and Gibson, V. (1982) *Liaison Groups in Early Education*. London, Schools Council.

Curtis, A. (1992) *Early Childhood Education Explained*. London, OMEP.

DES (1990) 'Starting with quality: Report of the Committee of Inquiry into the educational experiences offered to three and four year olds (Rumbold Report)'. London, HMSO.

DoH (1991) *The Children Act 1989: Guidance and Regulations*. London, HMSO.

Education, Science and Arts Committee (House of Commons) (1988) 'Educational provision for the under fives'. London, HMSO.

Pugh, G. (1988) *Services for Under Fives: Developing a Co-ordinated Approach*. London, NCB.

—— (ed.) (1992) *Contemporary Issues in the Early Years*. London, Paul Chapman, NCB.

Sheffield City Council (1986) 'It's their future'. Sheffield, Sheffield City Council.

—— (1991) 'Quality criteria for registration, inspection. Review in day care and education for under fives'. Sheffield, Sheffield, LEA.

—— (1992) 'Corporate childcare strategy, options for change'. Sheffield, Sheffield City Council.

Sheffield LEA (1986) 'Nursery education'. Sheffield, Sheffield LEA (reprinted 1992).

—— (1987) 'Early education'. Sheffield, Sheffield LEA (reprinted 1992).

—— (1988) 'Fun together'. Sheffield, Sheffield LEA.

—— (1991) 'Record keeping for children under five in all settings'. Sheffield, Sheffield LEA.

Chapter 15

Postscript. Supporting children and families – an optimistic future?

Tricia David

We live in a post-industrial society in which we have become more and more aware of the need to maximise the talents of our citizens, so women's expertise is to be valued and utilised, and children educated and cared for in ways which will foster optimal development. At the same time, we are becoming aware that the traditional structure of working lives denies those in work, and their children, the benefits of greater participation in childrearing. Young parents have become more isolated from their extended families because of high levels of mobility, so it seems likely that that the young families of today require more than ever, the support they lack as a result of the distances between family members, in order to fulfil the functions of the family discussed in the first chapter. In the past, childbirth would be spread over a number of years, so most older children would have been experienced in looking after younger relatives. Today, most children in a family are born within a few years of each other, and few 'new' mothers or fathers will have had extensive experience with babies. For the well-being of all concerned, strong networks of supportive services are vital.

But how can workers from the statutory and voluntary agencies provide effectively in the present system of market approaches, with the legal shifts and contradictions discussed by the writers in this book? Is a climate born out of a belief in competition an appropriate one in which to attempt to raise the next generation, or should the whole of society regard this as a serious, cooperative venture – children are, after all, our future citizens?

Working sensitively with parents and children is a complex and demanding task. It requires high levels of commitment, because frequent changes disrupt developing relationships, and high levels of training, because of its very complexity. The fact that training in this field is often regarded as unnecessary or basic is because of comparisons with parenthood and because it has traditionally been women's work. However, we have witnessed the effects of untrained social workers, in many of the recent scandals centred on children's homes; we know from research that the better educated those who work with children in education and daycare facilities, the better the learning and achievement of the children (Whitebrook *et al.* 1990); and who would dare to suggest that children could make do with less well-qualified health workers than are assigned to older members of the population?

If we are not to have an overhaul of the current system, but simply a laissez-faire attitude promulgated by a belief in the market and private sector development, if we are not to have one department to create the conditions necessary for true coordination and collaboration, then what are the possible constraints and challenges facing more effective service 'delivery'?

Many of the different services are provided by professionals and volunteers who come from different organisations, administered by different departments, with different structures, histories, philosophies and identities. Thus, the need for greater mutual understanding, for more opportunities for dialogue between different groups, through the provision of multi-professional courses is an important way forward. Such courses and dialogue require commitment by central and local government, by managers, and by individual workers, because they are time-consuming, as well as costly. Courses which include shadowing exercises can be fruitful, although in some cases this has been impossible, because of views about confidentiality. While this is a very important issue, and one which more workers engaging with families should debate, ways need to be found to avoid this becoming simply an excuse for preventing others from gaining an insight into a particular service. Probably the greatest barriers to the exchange of knowledge and practices are confidence and competence, and these can only be acquired through in-depth training in one's own role, and recognition by society of one's contribution. Such recognition involves pay and conditions of service, status in comparison with other professionals, further development of one's knowledge base through education up to and including higher degree level, and an active, well-funded research network. Monica Deigman (1993) draws attention to the dearth of university chairs in Early

Childhood Studies, and related subjects. She compares this with the number of professors of Sport Science recently appointed in Sweden, and argues that we can tell from this that young children and their parents seem, therefore, to be of little importance to society.

Finally, as many of the contributing authors have pointed out, provision for young children requires an adequate level of funding. Levels of poverty among children are more acute than in previous periods (Bradshaw 1990). If we do believe that this period of life is one of the most crucial, then we should be investing in it. As Mia Kellmer Pringle wrote two decades ago:

> A willingness to devote adequate resources to the care of children is the hallmark of a civilised society, as well as an investment in our future.
>
> (Pringle 1975: 148)

REFERENCES

Bergman, M. (1993) 'Early childcare and education in Sweden', in T. David (ed.) *Educational Provision for our Youngest Children: European Perspectives*. London, Paul Chapman.

Bradshaw, J. (1990) *Child Poverty and Deprivation in the UK*. London, NCB.

Pringle, M.K. (1975) *The Needs of Children*. London, Hutchinson.

Whitebrook, M., Howes, C. and Phillips, D. (1990) *Who Cares? Childcare Workers and the Quality of Care. Final Report of the National Childcare Staffing Study*. Berkeley, CA, Child Care Employee Project.

Name index

Abbot, P. 2
Adult Education Service 175–6
Alison 127–8
Athey, C. 40, 41, 151

Baldwin, N. xix, 104–18, 134
Barton, Councillor 172
Bebbington, A. 120
Bedfordshire 63
Ben 36–7
Bergman, M. 183
Bickler, G.J. xviii
Billingham, K. 23
Birchall, B. 31
Blackburn, C. xix, 1–25
Body Shop 75
Brandon, M. 122
Brazil 146
Bristol University 126
British Association for Early
    Childhood Education
    (BAECE) 48, 62
British Rail 74
Bronfenbrenner, U. xvi
Brown, M. xix, 47–65
Bruner, J. xvi
Business and Technical Council
    166
Byrne, E.A. 83

Calder, P. 165
Cambridgeshire 63
Central Council for the Education
    and Training of Social
    Workers (CCETSW) 166

Child Care Association 73
Child Support Agency 7
Childminding in Business 32
Children in Need 58
City Action Teams 71
City Challenge 71
City and Guilds 166
Cochran, M. 8
Cohen, B. 9
Colwell, M. 104, 119
Co-operative Bank 75
Council for the Accreditation of
    Teacher Education (CATE)
    162–3, 166
Council for Early Years Awards
    (CEYA) 167
Courtney 36–7
Cunningham-Burley, S. 8
Curtis, A. xx, 73, 159–69

Dahlstrom, E. 2
David, T. 1–11, 133–42, 161,
    182–4
Davie, Professor R. 134
Davie, Professor R. 134
De'Ath, E. xix, 93–103
Denmark 168
Department of Education and
    Science (DES) 146, 149, 170
Department of Health and
    Social Security (DHSS) 51,
    104, 107, 113, 115, 127, 149,
    171
Department of Social Services
    146
Donaldson, M. xvi

Dunn, J. 8

Early Childhood Unit *see*
    National Children's Bureau
Early Education Forum 48
Eastern Europe 129
Education Advisory Service 175
European Childcare Network
    138
European Parents Association
    (EPA) 48
Exley Playgroup 56

Family Health Service Authority
    17
Farmer, E. 124
Ferri, E. 31
Fletcher, C. 145
Fraser, N. 9
Freeman, M. 105
Freud, S. 119
Froebel Early Education Project
    40

Germany 168
Gil, D. 106
Gill, O. 111
Goldstein, J. 119
Graham, H. 4

Harrison, C. xix, 104–18, 134
Health Authority 174, 181
Health Visitors Association 133
Henley Safe Children Project 111
Herbert, E. xix, 6, 81–92
Hevey, D. 56, 73, 159, 161
Holman, R. 120
Holtermann, 8, 9, 70, 75
Home Office 113
House of Commons Select
    Committee 145

Italy 146

Jackson, B. and S. 28
Jackson, S. 119–32, 135
Jason 127
Joint Awarding Body (JAB) 167

Kelly, J.B. 96

Kendrick, C. 8
Kiddicare 74

Lambert, L. 119
Law Reform Group for
    Children's Daycare 48, 62
Lloyd, E. 4

Marshall, U. 147
Mayall, B. 28
Melhuish, E. 74
Midland Bank nursery 75
Miles, J. 120
Mitterauer, M. 2, 3
Mooni 36–7
Mosborough Townships Under
    Fives Service 173
Moss, P. 5, 74

National Association for the
    Education of Young Children
    64
National Child Development
    Study 119
National Childbirth Trust (NCT)
    61
National Childminding
    Association (NCMA) 26, 28,
    31–2, 54, 61, 75, 166
National Children's Bureau xvii,
    xviii, 134, 165
National Health Service
    Occupational Standards 166
National Private Day Nurseries
    Association 68
National Vocational
    Qualifications in Child Care
    and Education 73, 166–8
North America 126
Nursery Nurse Examination
    Board 166
Nutbrown, C. xix, 35–46

O'Neill, Dennis 119

Packman, J. 122–3
Papua New Guinea 146
Parker, R.A. 124
Parton, N. 105, 113
Pen Green Family Centre 37

Petrie, P. 28
Phoenix, A. 4, 5
Preschool Playgroups
    Association (PPA) xix, 48,
    52–3, 62, 64, 75, 166, 174
Pringle, M.K. 184
Pugh, G. xvii, xviii, 8, 173, 180

Reason, P. 147
Rowe, J. 119
Rubin, Z. 8
Rumbold Committee 138, 159,
    161
Rural Social Partnership 71
Rutter, M. 95, 96

Scottish Childminding
    Association (SCMA) 32
Select Committee see House of
    Commons
Sharp, A. xx, 170–81
Sheffield 170–81
Sheffield City Council 181
Shell 75
Sieder, R. 2, 3
Solity, J.E. xviii
Solnit, A.J. 119
Sothebys 75
Special Needs Consortium 134
Stuart 41
Sweden 5

Task Force Urban Programme 71
Thomas Cook 75

Thomas Coram Research Unit
    project 28–9, 74
Toynbee, P. 49

Under Fives Advisory
    Committee 179–80
United States 129–30

Voluntary Organisations Liaison
    Council for Under Fives
    (VOLCUF) 48
Vygotsky, L. xvi, 40, 136

Wallerstein, J.S. 96
Warner, J. xix, 26–34, 139
Warnock, Baroness 134
Warwickshire County Council
    Social Services Department 32
Wattam, C. 113
Webb, N.B. 6, 8
Welsh Development Agency 71
Whalley, M. xx, 135, 145–58
White, D.G. 6
Whittingham, V. xix, 66–77, 139
Woodhead, M. xvi
Woollett, E.A. 4, 5, 6
Working for Childcare 70, 74
World Organisation for Early
    Childhood Education
    (OMEP) 48
Wyton Playgroup 57

Young Persons Sub-committee
    180

Subject index

abuse, child 106, 129, 135; in
    foster care 126; investigation
    of 107, 112–14; prevention of
    109–10, 135, 148, 155;
    response to 114; role of police
    113
achievement, academic 46
accommodation, child provision
    109, 123
accredited prior learning 165–6
admission, to under-fives
    provision 174
adoption 120, 124–8
adventure, in play 137
ancestor worship 3
assertion, child 37–8
assessment 110–14

'babysitters', role of 8
behaviour, boys 137
bonding, with parents 6
bulk-buy facility 53, 63

care: children in xx, 119–32; and
    education see educare; factors
    predisposing to 120; multiple
    6; numbers in 121; preschool
    see daycare; quality see
    quality; requirement for 67
challenge, in play 137, 152
Child Care and Education,
    National Vocational
    Qualifications (NVQs) 56,
    162, 166–8
child: care see care; development

126, 164–5, 183; health see
    health; protection 3, 22, 104,
    107, 112–14, 148, 150–1, 154–5
Childline 140
childminding xix, 26–34, 130,
    139; conditions of work 30–1;
    support for 31–4
Children Act 1989 xv, xvi, xvii,
    xx, 5, 20, 27, 31, 33, 45, 48, 58,
    60, 62–4, 67–9, 71, 94–5, 101,
    104–9, 111–16, 119–23, 125,
    129–30, 133, 136–7, 160,
    167–8, 175–6, 180; Report
    1992 121
Children and Young Persons
    Act 1969 120
Children's Departments 119
choice see diversity
Cleveland Enquiry 126
collaboration, multi-disciplinary
    62–3; see also coordination
combined centres see daycare
communication, by teachers 164
community health see health
conciliation service 95
confidence 46; see also self-esteem
conflict, resolution of 96
constancy, in under-fives
    provision 6
contact order 94
continuity xx, 29, 59, 164; home
    and nursery 41; see also
    constancy
contracting out 72
cooperation see coordination

coordination, of services xx, xv,
    xvii, xviii, 15, 23, 62, 91, 113,
    161, 168, 170–81, 182–4
cost *see* funding
counselling 57, 165
creches 51
crisis intervention 114
cultural function, of family 3
culture, influence of xvi
curriculum 38–43, 50; daycare
    151, 155, 174–5; see also
    National Curriculum
Curtis Report 119

daycare xx, 5, 8–9, 50, 66–77,
    129–30, 145–59, 168;
    combined centres 145–58,
    173–4; insufficient 148; local
    authority provision 109, 137,
    145–58, 170–81; parental links
    154–6; role of 150, 156; survey
    70; in war years 146
depression, in mothers 5, 22, 129
deprivation model 155
development: child xvi, 45;
    cognitive 38, 41; personal 56,
    164, 168
developmental: needs, child 137,
    138; patterns 40; *see also*
    schema
disabilities: playgroup provision
    51; register of 109; *see also*
    handicap
disease, prevention 18
District Health Authorities
    (DHAs) 16–17
diversity, in under-fives
    provision 152, 159, 172
divorce *see* separation
Down's syndrome 81–92
drop-in centres 51

economic function, of family 3
economics, of care *see* funding
educare xx, 135, 140–1, 145–6,
    156, 159, 161–4, 166, 171–2
education: and care *see* educare;
    early years 160–6; importance
    of 128; inadequate 106;
    nursery *see* nursery;

preschool 8–9, 35–46, 50; role
    of playgroups in 52; service
    162, 170, 174
Education Acts 58: Bill 1993 134;
    Reform Act 1988 160, 172,
    173–5, 180; Schools Act 1992
    180
educator *see* educare
Emergency Protection Orders
    122
employers' role, in child care
    71–6
enabler 43
equal opportunities 58, 136–7
European Social Fund 71
expenses, needs for 63

facilitator 43
family: adequacy of 8; centres
    109, 130, 173; changes in 9;
    definition of 1–4; diversity of
    2; dynamics 89–91; forms of
    2; functions of xviii, 2–3;
    preservation 119; religious
    function of 3; reproductive
    function of 3; stress 150;
    support for xv; tree 98;
    uniqueness of 1–11; *see also*
    stepfamilies
fathers, role of 6–7, 84–90
feminist theory 4
finance *see* funding
flexibility, of care 138, 172
foster care 121, 123–5
friends, importance of 8
fund: holding 16–17; raising 60
funding: of care 9, 50, 62, 64,
    70–1, 148, 180, 184; NHS 160

gender, impact on upbringing 4
general practitioner 83, 89, 133;
    contract 16–17
GEST Activity 175
grandparents, importance of 8

handicap, disclosure of 82–7
harm: *see* abuse; *see also*
    significant harm
health: behaviour 18; care
    practitioners 15; child 22, 45,

159; community profiling
19–20, 23; of the nation 24;
promotion work 20–4; public
23–4, 58; and safety 50, 58,
137; service *see* NHS; visitors
xix, 15–25, 50, 57, 83, 89, 133
Health Services and Public
Health Act 1968 27
Home-Start 54
homophobia 111
hospital play: schemes 50; work
166
housing, inadequate 106
humanity 46
hygiene 50

ill-treatment *see* abuse
in need, children *see* need
inclusive fostering *see* foster care
information 178; accessibility of
91; lack of 84, 87–9
injury *see* abuse
interaction: adult–child 137;
child–peergroup 137
investigation 114
involvement, child 137
isolation 129, 141

joint centres *see* daycare,
combined

language 136
law *see* legislation
leadership *see* management
learning: child xvi, 42, 151, 164–5;
continuous 56; opportunity
138; support and structure of
137; *see also* development
legalism 113
legislation 160; on childminding
27–8; on daycare 67;
educational xvii, 160;
employment 58; health 160;
on playgroups 58–61; relating
to under-fives 160, 164, 180;
social work 113; *see also*
Children Act; Education Acts
liaison work 63, 177–8; *see also*
coordination
listening skills 91

local authorities: assistance by
109; requirements of 137; *see
also* social workers
Looking After Children scheme
127–8

management 164–5
manners 153
market forces, inappropriateness
of 76
maternity provision 76
mediation service 95
mental illness 129; *see also*
depression
mother–child bond 4; reaction to
handicap 82–4
motherhood, status of 5
multi-professionalism 43–5
musical activities 50

National Curriculum 42, 58, 139,
151, 160, 162–3, 175
National Health Service 15; and
Community Care Act 1990
16, 17, 180; trusts 17; *see also*
health
National Vocational
Qualifications (NVQs) *see*
Child Care and Education
need: children in 59, 104–18,
133–42, 160; concept of xix;
definition of 108, 110; related
18–19; special 81–92, 166–7, 171
neglect: contributory factors 129;
prevention of 109
negotiation 152
networking 91, 176–7; *see also*
coordination
Nurseries and Childminders'
Regulations Act 1948 27, 50
nursery: costs of 148; day *see*
daycare; education 66–77,
133–4, 140, 149, 151, 170–1;
nurses 53; nursing 161, 166;
private 66–77; provision xix,
134, 145; school 48, 130;
setting up 68–71

Opportunities for Volunteering
Scheme 51

opportunity, equality of 43
organisation, importance of 137

paramountcy, of child welfare
    see welfare
parental: confidence 110; duties
    xv, 1; involvement 137; leave
    76; rights 122; responsibilities
    see responsibility; role,
    importance of xviii
parenting 9; diminished ability
    for 96
partnership 21, 71–6, 107,
    115–16, 123
pathologising, of families 149
patriarchal model 2
peer-relations, importance of 8
permanency planning 121
Place of Safety Orders 121–2
play 43; discovery 43;
    experimental 43; exploratory
    43; free 152; imaginative 137;
    structured 153
playgroups *see* preschool play
    groups
policing *see* social policing
polyadic xvi
Poor Law 119
potty-training 153
poverty 21, 106, 111, 129
power 116
premises: for daycare 69; for
    playgroups 59
preschool playgroups xix, 47–65,
    130, 140, 171; administration
    50; for forces children 51; in
    hostels 51; prison 50;
    working in 56–8
primary schools; preparation
    for 58; under-fives admission
    174
probation officers 133
progress, children's 164
prohibitive steps order 94
protective function: of daycare
    148, 151, 154–5; of family 3; of
    social work 104; *see also* child
    protection
psychologists 53
psychology, of childbirth 1

qualifications *see* training
quality: of care 64, 73–5, 125–8,
    137–9, 159, 166, 172, 175–6; of
    education 64; of foster care
    125–8; kitemark of 74;
    organisation, role in 137; of
    playgroups 175–6
questioning 152

racism 106, 111, 136, 167
reforms, governmental xvii
regeneration programmes 71
regional variation, in childcare
    provision 66–7
regionalisation 54
registration, of daycare centres
    67–8, 73, 160, 176
relationships, formation of 8
rescue, child 119, 135
residence order 94
residential care 166
respect, for children 164
respite care 123
responsibility: family 3, 123;
    legal 113; local authority
    108–9; parental xv, 122; social
    workers 113; state 3
return home 123
reunion *see* return home
rights: of children 107, 112; of
    parents 112
rising five admission *see*
    primary schools
rotation 41
Rumbold Report 136, 171

safety *see* health and safety
schema 40–3
security, emotional 36
selecting 42
self-esteem, childhood 36, 152
separation 93–5; affect on
    children xix, 95–102; anxiety
    153
sexism 106, 111, 136, 167
Short Report 104
siblings, importance of 8
significant harm 134–6
size, effect of group 137
social: contacts 51; development

37, 151; interaction 37; justice
136; policing 21–2; policy 165;
service departments 145–58,
162, 174, 176
social work xix; entry to
profession 165; transition in 122
social workers 53, 104–18, 133;
role of 105, 108–10
socialising function, of family 3
sorting 42
special needs see need
specific needs order 94
stability, of care 29, 36
standards, occupational 167; see
also quality
status, for preschool teachers 168
stepfamilies 94, 99–101
stimulation 152, 155
substitute care see care
support 43; for children and
families 104, 182–4; for
parents 123–5; for playgroups
53
surveillance, by social workers
109

table manners see manners
teachers 53; career progression
see development; early years
161–4, 168
teaching: entry to profession
165; skills 42
toddler groups 50
toy-loan schemes 53

training: for childminders 29–30;
for daycare work 73, 109, 137,
156; for educare 165–8, 183;
multi-disciplinary 62–3; for
nursing 161, 166; for
playgroup organisers 50,
53–6, 60; for presentation of
handicap 91; for social
workers 161–2; for work with
young children 159–69, 175,
183
Training and Enterprise
Councils (TECs) 70–1

umbrella organisations 48, 62
under-fives 171; initiative 51, 64;
provision xv, xvii–xx, 48, 62,
159, 172, 180; see also
preschool

voluntary organisations 47–65;
partnership with statutory
agencies 64

war, and daycare 146
Warnock Report 81
welfare, child 137; education
officers 133; intervention 104,
127; paramountcy of 107, 114,
116, 167; system 119–32; see
also need
workplace nurseries 72

zone of proximal development 40